Randall House Minister's Manual

written and compiled by

Billy A. Melvin

KJV Edition

randall house

Second Edition

Printed in the United States of America.

CONTENTS

1

General Rules for Conducting Public Worship

1. *Aim at quality rather than quantity.* Never let a service drag. Close the meeting as soon as all the vital parts of the program have been covered.

2. *Always offer good music.* It is better to have no music than poor music. In fact, poor music distracts from worship. Most churches would be better off with one good soloist than with the second-rate quartets or choirs that they use.

3. *Public prayer should be brief and inspirational.* The Lord's Prayer contains only seventy words, which can be uttered in less than thirty seconds. Dean Charles R. Brown says, "The Master condemned the long-winded, ostentatious prayer . . . He insisted that every prayer should be a simple, direct, and genuine transaction between the soul of the man and God." Dwight L. Moody said, "If you can't pray short prayers, why, don't pray at all. These men who make long prayers are generally the ones that pray least at home. They are generally prayerless prayers, and they take the spirit right out of the meeting."

The essential purpose of public prayer is to lead the congregation into a prayerful mood. Therefore, it must be inspirational. Dr. John Balcom Shaw gave the following suggestion to those who lead in public prayer: "Put your heart in command, not your mind; and let your lips breathe only that which rises up within you there. Spurgeon's prayers were as wonderful as any I ever heard. They were unmistakably the outgoings of a soul in the presence of its God."

4. *Use the "grand old hymns" but have a warm welcome for the new ones too.* It is important to get everybody singing. It can be done by selecting popular Christian hymns and songs, old and new, which are popular because they blend good music with excellent biblical lyrics. Of the many thousands of Christian hymns and songs in the world only several hundred are universal favorites. Select your hymns and songs carefully and be sure they are accompanied by tunes that can be sung by the people.

5. *Never permit your preaching to become a bore.* Preaching is too complicated a subject to be discussed here. Let it be enough to quote from one of America's most popular preachers. "The only kind of a sermon which a man can preach successfully, is the kind which suits his own personality." Find out which kind of preaching you can do well enough to hold a crowd's interest, then stick to it. The crowd will keep coming. Moreover, find out how long you can talk and still be interesting. Don't speak a second longer. The average preacher is a twenty-minute man. He will not attempt long sermons if he is wise.

6. *Make the communion service a distinctively family gathering with the Savior as the host.* All those who know and love the Savior should be welcomed regardless of their formal creed or church connection.

7. *Finally, put enthusiasm into every part of every service.* In the different parts of the service there should be nothing dull or boring. Coldness and formality cause re-

ligious worship to have no value. Take time to put meaning into every act of worship—prayer, responsive reading, sermon, singing, and announcements. Remember the words addressed to Ian Maclaren, "Your best work, in the pulpit, has been to put heart into men for the coming week."

2
Church—Pastor Relationship

Getting off to a good start

Before arriving on the field:

1. Respond to a church's call with humility and enthusiasm, understanding the seriousness and privilege of ministry.
2. Ask for prayer.
3. Answer all letters. A general letter to all members of the congregation is a good idea.
4. Begin to pray for the church. Establish a prayer list to pray for members by name.
5. Get an up-to-date copy of the church roll.
6. Begin to think through your planning for this particular church.

After arriving on the field:

1. Do not brag or promote yourself.
2. Under normal circumstances, don't outline any ambitious program too quickly.
3. Be characterized by simplicity, humility, friendliness, and spiritual power.
4. Launch into the work as if you intend to stay the rest of your life.
5. If you want to make rapid progress, go *slow.*
6. Don't make any major changes for six months. It will take at least that long to get to know the people and begin to earn their trust.

7. Get acquainted with the people in the church and community.
8. Be careful how you relate to and speak about your predecessor.

General suggestions for a happy pastoral relationship

1. Be a leader and not a dictator.
2. Recruit and equip others to help do the work. Don't do everything yourself.
3. Insist on regular meetings with your deacons, trustees and other leaders in the church.
4. Don't claim to know everything or insist that everything be done your way. Laymen can have good ideas too.
5. Commend your people as often as possible, and always when it is deserved. Don't always address them as if they fall short of your expectations.
6. Spend sufficient time each week in the study of God's Word. Your people will expect to be fed. Feed them.
7. Let the Holy Spirit, through the Word, guide people into steps of spiritual progress. Progress should not be dependant upon human effort apart from the work of the Spirit.
8. Make wise use of your time. Don't waste it. It will quickly become obvious if you are not a hard worker.
9. Visit the families of your church as well as the prospects. Balance outreach and care for present members.

10. Never betray the confidence of a member. If you do, you have probably destroyed any possibility of a future counseling ministry.
11. Never allow yourself to be alone with any member of the opposite sex.
12. Take responsibility for the leadership and welfare of your home. Congregations will not long respect a pastor who is not the loving leader of his home.
13. Pay your debts. Failure to do so will soon kill any possibility of a successful ministry.
14. Keep the church fully informed about the finances. If a budget is adopted, honor it.
15. Set up a system of financial accountability to protect you and the church from the possibility or accusation of the misuse of finances.
16. Seek to keep finances from being an unreasonable burden or distraction in the life of the church.
17. Be known as a "man of God."

When leaving a church

1. Never use a threat of resignation in an attempt to get a raise in salary or win a power struggle.
2. If you have enjoyed a good relationship with your deacons, it is usually wise to share your decision with them shortly before resigning.
3. Write out your resignation and read it to the entire church.
4. Once you have resigned—leave!

3

Christian Baptism

Suggestions

Prior to the baptismal service, the minister should speak with each candidate, explaining the significance and meaning of the ordinance. He should let the candidate know what to expect and confirm the time and place of the baptism. The minister should take this opportunity to stress the importance of membership in the church. He should instruct the candidate to wear suitable clothing of a modest nature or an appropriate baptismal robe. The baptismal service should usually be part of, or follow a Sunday worship service, or be at a time and place which allows as many members of the church as possible to witness the baptism. It is wise to baptize an individual soon after his conversion.

One or more of the following Scriptures may be read before the minister descends into the water.

I

In those days came John the Baptist, preaching in the wilderness of Judaea, And saying, Repent ye: for the kingdom of heaven is at hand. For this is he that was spoken of by the prophet Esaias, saying, The voice of one crying in the wilderness, Prepare ye the way of the Lord, make his paths straight. And the same John had his raiment of camel's hair, and a leather girdle about his loins;

and his meat was locusts and wild honey. Then went out to him Jerusalem, and all Judaea, and all the region round about Jordan. And were baptized of him in Jordan, confessing their sins. But when he saw many of the Pharisees and Sadducees come to his baptism, he said unto them, O generation of vipers, who hath warned you to flee from the wrath to come? Bring forth therefore fruits meet for repentance: And think not to say within yourselves, We have Abraham to our father: for I say unto you, that God is able of these stones to raise up children unto Abraham. And now also the axe is laid unto the root of the trees: therefore every tree which bringeth not forth good fruit is hewn down, and cast into the fire. I indeed baptize you with water unto repentance: but he that cometh after me is mightier than I, whose shoes I am not worthy to bear: he shall baptize you with the Holy Ghost, and with fire: Whose fan is in his hand, and he will thoroughly purge his floor, and gather his wheat into the garner; but he will burn up the chaff with unquenchable fire. Then cometh Jesus from Galilee to Jordan unto John, to be baptized of him. But John forbade him, saying, I have need to be baptized of thee, and comest thou to me? And Jesus answering said unto him, Suffer it to be so now: for thus it becometh us to fulfill all righteousness. Then he suffered him. And Jesus, when he was baptized, went up straightway out of the water: and, lo, the heavens were opened unto him, and he saw the Spirit of God descending like a dove, and lighting upon him: And lo a voice from heaven, saying, This is my beloved Son, in whom I am well pleased.

—Matthew 3:1-17

II

The beginning of the gospel of Jesus Christ, the Son of God; As it is written in the prophets, Behold, I send my messenger before thy face, which shall prepare thy way before thee. The voice of one crying in the wilderness, Prepare ye the way of the Lord, make his paths straight. John did baptize in the wilderness, and preach the baptism of repentance for the remission of sins. And there went out unto him all the land of Judaea, and they of Jerusalem, and were all baptized of him in the river of Jordan, confessing their sins. And John was clothed with camel's hair, and with a girdle of a skin about his loins; and he did eat locusts and wild honey; And preached saying, There cometh one mightier than I after me, the latchet of whose shoes I am not worthy to stoop down and unloose. I indeed have baptized you with water: but he shall baptize you with the Holy Ghost. And it came to pass in those days, that Jesus came from Nazareth of Galilee, and was baptized of John in Jordan. And straightway coming up out of the water, he saw the heavens opened, and the Spirit like a dove descending upon him: And there came a voice from heaven, saying, Thou art my beloved Son in whom I am well pleased.

—Mark 1:1-11

And Jesus came and spake unto them, saying, All power is given unto me in heaven and in earth. Go ye therefore, and teach all nations, baptizing them in the name of the Father, and of the Son, and of the Holy Ghost: Teaching them to observe all things whatsoever I have commanded you: and, lo, I am with you alway, even unto the end of the world. Amen.

—Matthew 28:18-20

Afterward he appeared unto the eleven as they sat at meat, and upbraided them with their unbelief and hardness of heart, because they believed not them which had seen him after he was risen. And he said unto them, Go ye into all the world, and preach the gospel to every creature. He that believeth and is baptized shall be saved; but he that believeth not shall be damned.

—Mark 16:14-16

Then Peter said unto them, Repent, and be baptized every one of you in the name of Jesus Christ for the remission of sins, and ye shall receive the gift of the Holy Ghost. For the promise is unto you, and to your children, and to all that are afar off, even as many as the Lord our God shall call. And with many other words did he testify and exhort, saying, Save yourselves from this untoward generation. Then they that gladly received his word were baptized: and the same day there were added unto them about three thousand souls. And they continued steadfastly in the apostles' doctrine and fellowship, and in breaking of bread, and in prayers.

—Acts 2:38-42

III

And the angel of the Lord spake unto Philip, saying, Arise, and go toward the south unto the way that goeth down from Jerusalem unto Gaza, which is desert. And he arose and went: and, behold, a man of Ethipoia, an eunuch of great authority under Candace queen of the Ethiopians, who had the charge of all her treasure, and had come to Jerusalem for to worship, Was returning, and sitting in his chariot read Esaias the prophet. Then the Spirit said unto Philip, Go near, and join thyself to this chariot. And Philip ran thither to him, and heard him read the prophet Esaias, and said, Understandest thou what thou readest? And he said, How can I, except some man should guide me? And he desired Philip that he would come up and sit with him. The place of the scripture which he read was this, He was led as a sheep to the slaughter; and like a lamb dumb before his shearer, so opened he not his mouth: In his humiliation his judgment was taken away: and who shall declare his generation: for his life is taken from the earth. And the eunuch answered Philip, and said, I pray thee, of whom speaketh the prophet this? of himself, or of some other man? Then Philip opened his mouth, and began at the same scripture, and preached unto him Jesus. And as they went on their way, they came unto a certain water: and the eunuch said, See, here is water; what doth hinder me to be baptized? And Philip said, If thou believest with all thine heart, thou mayest. And he answered and said, I believe that Jesus Christ is the Son of God. And he commanded the chariot to stand still: and they went down both into the water, both Philip and the eunuch; and he baptized him. And when they were come up out of the water, the Spirit of the Lord caught away Philip, that the eunuch saw him no more: and he went on his way rejoicing.

—Acts 8:26-39

While Peter yet spake these words, the Holy Ghost fell on all them which heard the word. And they of the circumcision which believed were astonished, as many as came with Peter, because that on the Gentiles also was poured out the gift of the Holy Ghost. For they heard them speak with tongues, and magnify God. Then answered Peter, Can any man forbid water, that these should not be baptized, which have received the Holy Ghost as well as we? And he commanded them to be baptized in the name of the Lord. Then prayed they him to tarry certain days.

—Acts 10:44-48

IV

And at midnight Paul and Silas prayed, and sang praises unto God: and the prisoners heard them. And suddenly there was a great earthquake, so that the foundations of the prison were shaken: and immediately all the doors were opened, and every one's bands were loosed. And the keeper of the prison awaking out of his sleep, and seeing the prison doors open, he drew out his sword, and would have killed himself, supposing that the prisoners had been fled. But Paul cried with a loud voice, saying, Do thyself no harm: for we are all here. Then he called for a light, and sprang in, and came trembling, and fell down before Paul and Silas, And brought them out, and said, Sirs, what must I do to be saved? And they said, Believe on the Lord Jesus Christ, and thou shalt be saved, and thy house. And they spake unto him the word of the Lord, and to all that were in his house. And he took them the same hour of the night, and washed their stripes; and was baptized, he and all his, straightway. And when he had brought them into his house, he set meat before them, and rejoiced, believing in God with all his house.

—Acts 16:25-34

V

What shall we say then? Shall we continue in sin, that grace may abound? God forbid. How shall we, that are dead to sin, live any longer therein? Know ye not, that so many of us as were baptized into Jesus Christ were baptized into his death? Therefore we are buried with him by baptism into death: that like as Christ was raised up from the dead by the glory of the Father, even so we also should walk in newness of life. For if we have been planted together in the likeness of his death, we shall be also in the likeness of his resurrection: Knowing this, that our old man is crucified with him, that the body of sin might be destroyed, and henceforth we should not serve sin. For he that is dead is freed from sin. Now if we be dead with Christ, we believe that we shall also live with him: Knowing that Christ being raised from the dead dieth no more; death hath no more dominion over him. For in that he died, he died unto sin once: but in that he liveth, he liveth unto God. Likewise reckon ye also yourselves to be dead indeed unto sin, but alive unto God through Jesus Christ our Lord.

—Romans 6:1-11

After reading a selection of Scripture, the minister may make appropriate remarks to the congregation and offer prayer. If desired, the following statement may be used.

Dear church family and friends, from the time of the Apostles the church has regarded baptism as the outward and visible sign of an inward and spiritual reality. Water baptism does not save us or wash away our sins.

It serves as an outward object lesson of what has taken place in our hearts through the work of the Holy Spirit when we believe in Christ and receive Him as Savior and Lord. It illustrates our death to sin and rising to walk in a new way of life. By presenting themselves to receive this holy ordinance, these believers are publicly proclaiming that they have received Christ as Savior and Lord, and that they intend to follow and live for Him for the rest of their lives with the help of the Holy Spirit.

When directed by the minister, each candidate will join the minister in the water and the minister shall say:

In humble obedience to the command of Christ, our Lord and Savior, I baptize you, my (brother / sister), in the name of the Father, and of the Son, and of the Holy Spirit. Amen.

or

Upon the profession of your faith, and in obedience to the command of Christ who is the Head of the Church, I now baptize you in the name of the Father, and of the Son, and of the Holy Spirit. Amen.

When the candidates have been baptized, prayer may be offered, a hymn or Christian song sung by the congregation, and a blessing or closing prayer pronounced by the minister.

4
The Lord's Supper

Suggestions

Prior to the Lord's Supper, the minister should meet with the deacons of the church to assure proper preparation for this sacred service. Each deacon should clearly understand his responsibility in the service so there is no confusion or uncertainty. The minister should refer to the elements as the *bread* and *cup.* At no time should this important service be rushed. Ample time should be allowed for participants to enter into the spirit of this ordinance. The church should practice this ordinance often enough for its membership to receive the blessing of such a service, but not so often that it becomes routine. An observance each quarter might be appropriate.

One or more of the following Scriptures may be read by the minister.

I

Now the first day of the feast of unleavened bread the disciples came to Jesus, saying unto him, Where wilt thou that we prepare for thee to eat the passover? And he said, Go into the city to such a man, and say unto him, The Master saith, My time is at hand; I will keep the passover at thy house with my disciples. And the disciples did as Jesus had appointed them; and they made ready the passover. Now when the even was come, he sat down with the twelve. And as they did eat, he said, Verily I say unto you, that one of you shall betray me. And they were exceeding sorrowful, and began every one of them to say unto him, Lord, is it I? And he answered and said, He that dippeth his hand with me in the dish, the same shall betray me. The Son of man goeth as it is written of him: but woe unto that man by whom the Son of man is betrayed! it had been good for that man if he had not been born. Then Judas, which betrayed him, answered and said, Master, is it I? He said unto him, Thou hast said. And as they were eating, Jesus took bread, and blessed it, and brake it, and gave it to the disciples, and said, Take, eat; this is my body. And he took the cup, and gave thanks, and gave it to them, saying, Drink ye all of it; For this is my blood of the new testament, which is shed for many for the remission of sins. But I say unto you, I will not drink henceforth of this fruit of the vine, until that day when I drink it new with you in my Father's kingdom. And when they had sung an hymn, they went out into the mount of Olives.

—Matthew 26:17-30

II

And the first day of unleavened bread, when they killed the passover, his disciples said unto him, Where wilt thou that we go and prepare that thou mayest eat the passover? And he sendeth forth two of his disciples, and saith unto them, Go ye into the city, and there shall meet you a man bearing a pitcher of water: follow him. And wheresoever he shall go in, say ye to the goodman of the house, The Master saith, Where is the guestchamber, where I shall eat the passover with my disciples? And he will shew you a large upper room furnished and prepared: there make ready for us. And his disciples went forth, and came into the city, and found as he had said unto them: and they made ready the passover. And in the evening he cometh with the twelve. And as they sat and did eat, Jesus said, Verily I say unto you, One of you which eateth with me shall betray me. And they began to be sorrowful, and to say unto him one by one, Is it I? and another said, Is it I? And he answered and said unto them, It is one of the twelve, that dippeth with me in the dish. The Son of man indeed goeth, as it is written of him: but woe to that man by whom the Son of man is betrayed! good were it for that man if he had never been born. And as they did eat, Jesus took bread, and blessed, and brake it, and gave to them, and said, Take, eat: this is my body. And he took the cup, and when he had given thanks, he gave it to them: and they all drank of it. And he said unto them, This is my blood of the new testament, which is shed for many. Verily I say unto you, I will drink no more of the fruit of the vine, until that day that I drink it new in the kingdom of God. And when they had sung an hymn, they went out into the mount of Olives.

—Mark 14:12-26

III

Then came the day of unleavened bread, when the passover must be killed. And he sent Peter and John, saying, Go and prepare us the passover, that we may eat. And they said unto him, Where wilt thou that we prepare? And he said unto them, Behold, when ye are entered into the city, there shall a man meet you, bearing a pitcher of water; follow him into the house where he entereth in. And ye shall say unto the goodman of the house, The Master saith unto thee, Where is the guest-chamber, where I shall eat the passover with my disciples? And he shall shew you a large upper room furnished: there make ready. And they went, and found as he had said unto them: and they made ready the passover. And when the hour was come, he sat down, and the twelve apostles with him. And he said unto them, With desire I have desired to eat this passover with you before I suffer: For I say unto you, I will not any more eat thereof, until it be fulfilled in the kingdom of God. And he took the cup, and gave thanks, and said, Take this, and divide it among yourselves: For I say unto you, I will not drink of the fruit of the vine, until the kingdom of God shall come. And he took bread, and gave thanks, and brake it, and gave unto them, saying, This is my body which is given for you: this do in remembrance of me. Likewise also the cup after supper, saying, This cup is the new testament in my blood, which is shed for you. But, behold, the hand of him that betrayeth me is with me on the table. And truly the Son of man goeth, as it was determined: but woe unto that man by whom he is betrayed!

—Luke 22:7-22

The minister shall make any remarks that are appropriate to the occasion, and invite every Christian present to participate in the Lord's Supper. The deacons should then uncover the communion table and the minister should take a bread tray in his hands and say:

The Lord Jesus, the same night in which he was betrayed took bread: And when he had given thanks, he broke it, and said, Take, eat: this is my body, which is broken for you: do this in remembrance of me.

At this time the minister may pray, or call upon any minister, or one of the deacons to pray. He will then pass the bread trays to the deacons for distribution among the congregation with the instruction that each participant hold the bread until all have been served. When the deacons have returned to the table, they are served by the minister, and one deacon, in turn, serves the minister. The minister should then say:

Let us eat together.

or

Let us eat to remind ourselves of Christ's body that was broken for us.

The minister should then take a cup tray in his hands and say:

In the same way He also took the cup after eating, saying, This cup is the new testament in my blood: do this, as often as you drink it, in remembrance of me.

At this time the minister may pray, or call upon any minister, or one of the deacons to pray. He will then pass the cup trays to the deacons for distribution among the congregation with the in-

struction that each participant hold the cup until all have been served. When the deacons have returned to the table, they should be served by the minister, and one deacon, in turn, should serve the minister. The minister should then say:

Let us drink together.

or

Let us drink to remind ourselves of Christ's blood that was shed to take away our sins.

It is now time to participate in the Washing of the Saints' Feet. If there are no communion cup holders on the pews, the cup trays could be passed again to collect the empty cups, or the participants be instructed to set the cups on the floor to be collected later. The communion table should be re-covered.

5
Washing the Saints' Feet

Suggestions

Prior to the observance of this ordinance, the minister should meet with the deacons of the church to assure proper preparation. Preparations should be made for men and women in separate rooms, or in a way that allows for proper privacy. This ordinance of the church is normally observed following the Lord's Supper.

One or more of the following Scriptures may be read by the minister.

I

Now before the feast of the passover, when Jesus knew that his hour was come that he should depart out of this world unto the Father, having loved his own which were in the world, he loved them unto the end. And supper being ended, the devil having now put into the heart of Judas Iscariot, Simon's son, to betray him; Jesus knowing that the Father had given all things into his hands, and that he was come from God, and went to God; He riseth from supper, and laid aside his garments; and took a towel, and girded himself. After that he poureth water into a bason, and began to wash the disciples' feet, and to wipe them with the towel wherewith he was girded. Then cometh he to Simon Peter: and Peter said unto him, Lord, dost thou wash my feet? Jesus answered and said unto him, What I do thou knowest not now; but thou shalt know hereafter. Peter saith unto him, Thou shalt never wash my feet. Jesus answered him, If I wash thee not, thou hast no part with me. Simon Peter said unto him, Lord, not my feet only, but also my hands and my head. Jesus saith to him, He that is washed needeth not save to wash his feet, but is clean every whit: and ye are clean, but not all. For he knew who should betray him; therefore said he, Ye are not all clean. So after he had washed their feet, and had taken his garments, and was set down again, he said unto them, Know ye what I have done to you? Ye call me Master and Lord: and ye say well; for so I am. If I then, your Lord and Master, have washed your feet; ye also ought to wash one another's feet. For I have given you an example, that ye should do as I have done to you. Verily, verily, I say unto you, The servant is not greater than his lord; neither he that is sent greater than he that sent him. If ye know these things, happy are ye if ye do them.

—John 13:1-17

II

I therefore, the prisoner of the Lord, beseech you that ye walk worthy of the vocation wherewith ye are called, With all lowliness and meekness, with longsuffering, forbearing one another in love; Endeavouring to keep the unity of the Spirit in the bond of peace. There is one body, and one Spirit, even as ye are called in one hope of your calling; One Lord, one faith, one baptism, One God and Father of all, who is above all, and through all, and in you all. But unto every one of us is given grace according to the measure of the gift of Christ. Wherefore he saith, When he ascended up on high, he led captivity captive, and gave gifts unto men. (Now that he ascended, what is it but that he also descended first into the lower parts of the earth? He that descended is the same also that ascended up far above all heavens, that he might fill all things.) And he gave some, apostles; and some, prophets; and some, evangelists; and some, pastors and teachers; For the perfecting of the saints, for the work of the ministry, for the edifying of the body of Christ: Till we all come in the unity of the faith, and of the knowledge of the Son of God, unto a perfect man, unto the measure of the stature of the fulness of Christ: That we henceforth be no more children, tossed to and fro, and carried about with every wind of doctrine, by the sleight of men, and cunning craftiness, whereby they lie in wait to deceive; But speaking the truth in love, may grow up into him in all things, which is the head, even Christ: From whom the whole body fitly joined together and compacted by that which every joint supplieth, according to the effectual working in the measure of every part, maketh increase of the body unto the edifying of itself in love. This I say therefore, and testify in the Lord, that ye henceforth walk not as other Gentiles walk, in the vanity of their mind, Having the understanding darkened, being alienated from the life of God through the ignorance that is in them, because of the blindness of their heart: Who being past feeling have given themselves over unto lasciviousness, to work all uncleanness with greediness. But ye have not so learned Christ; if so be that ye have heard him, and have been taught by him, as the truth is in Jesus: That ye put off concerning the former conversation the old man, which is corrupt according to the deceitful lusts; And be renewed in the spirit of your mind; And that ye put on the new man, which after God is created in righteousness and true holiness. Wherefore putting away lying, speak every man truth with his neighbour: for we are members one of another. Be ye angry, and sin not: let not the sun go down upon your wrath: Neither give place to the devil. Let him that stole steal no more: but rather let him labour, working with his hands the thing which is good, that he may have to give to him that needeth. Let no corrupt communication proceed out of your mouth, but that which is good to the use of edifying, that it may minister grace unto the hearers. And grieve not the holy Spirit of God, whereby ye are sealed unto the day of redemption. Let all bitterness, and wrath, and anger, and clamour, and evil speaking, be put away from you, with all malice: And be ye kind one to another, tenderhearted, forgiving one another, even as God for Christ's sake hath forgiven you.

—Ephesians 4

III

Behold, what manner of love the Father hath bestowed upon us, that we should be called the sons of God: therefore the world knoweth us not, because it knew him not. Beloved, now are we the sons of God, and it doth not yet appear what we shall be: but we know that, when he shall appear, we shall be like him; for we shall see him as he is. And every man that hath this hope in him purifieth himself, even as he is pure. Whosoever commiteth sin transgresseth also the law: for sin is the transgression of the law. And ye know that he was manifested to take away our sins; and in him is no sin. Whosoever abideth in him sinneth not: whosoever sinneth hath not seen him, neither known him. Little children, let no man deceive you: he that doeth righteousness is righteous, even as he is righteous. He that commiteth sin is of the devil; for the devil sinneth from the beginning. For this purpose the Son of God was manifested, that he might destroy the works of the devil. Whosoever is born of God doth not commit sin; for his seed remaineth in him: and he cannot sin, because he is born of God. In this the children of God are manifest, and the children of the devil: whosoever doeth not righteousness is not of God, neither he that loveth not his brother. For this is the message that ye heard from the beginning, that we should love one another. Not as Cain, who was of that wicked one, and slew his brother. And wherefore slew he him? Because his own works were evil, and his brother's righteous. Marvel not, my brethren, if the world hate you. We know that we have passed from death unto life, because we love the brethren. He that loveth not his brother abideth in death. Whosoever hateth his brother is a murderer: and ye know that no murderer hath eternal life abiding in him. Hereby perceive we the love of God, because he laid down his life for us: and we ought to lay down our lives for the brethren. But whoso hath this world's good, and seeth his brother have need, and shutteth up his bowels of compassion from him, how dwelleth the love of God in him? My little children, let us not love in word, neither in tongue; but in deed and in truth. And hereby we know that we are of the truth, and shall assure our hearts before him. For if our heart condemn us, God is greater than our heart, and knoweth all things. Beloved, if our heart condemn us not, then have we confidence toward God. And whatsoever we ask, we receive of him, because we keep his commandments, and do those things that are pleasing in his sight. And this is his commandment, That we should believe on the name of his Son Jesus Christ, and love one another, as he gave us commandment. And he that keepeth his commandments dwelleth in him, and he in him. And hereby we know that he abideth in us, by the Spirit which he hath given us.

—1 John 3

IV

Now in this that I declare unto you I praise you not, that ye come together not for the better, but for the worse. For first of all, when ye come together in the church, I hear that there be divisions among you; and I partly believe it. For there must be also heresies among you, that they which are approved may be made manifest among you. When ye come together therefore into one place, this is not to eat the Lord's supper. For in eating every one taketh before other his own supper: and one is hungry, and another in drunken. What? have ye not houses to eat and to drink in? or despise ye the church of God, and shame them that have not? What shall I say to you? shall I praise you in this? I praise you not. For I have received of the Lord that which also I delivered unto you, That the Lord Jesus the same night in which he was betrayed took bread: And when he had given thanks, he brake it, and said, Take eat: this is my body, which is broken for you: this do in remembrance of me. After the same manner also he took the cup, when he had supped, saying, This cup is the new testament in my blood: this do ye, as oft as ye drink it, in remembrance of me. For as often as ye eat this bread, and drink this cup, ye do shew the Lord's death till he come. Wherefore whosoever shall eat this bread, and drink this cup of the Lord, unworthily, shall be guilty of the body and blood of the Lord. But let a man examine himself, and so let him eat of that bread, and drink of that cup. For he that eateth and drinketh unworthily, eateth and drinketh damnation to himself, not discerning the Lord's body. For this cause many are weak and sickly among you, and many sleep. For if we would judge ourselves, we should not be judged. But when we are judged, we are chastened of the Lord, that we should not be condemned with the world. Wherefore, my brethren, when ye come together to eat, tarry one for another. And if any man hunger, let him eat at home; that ye come not together unto condemnation. And the rest will I set in order when I come.

—1 Corinthians 11:17-34

The minister shall make any remarks that are appropriate to the occasion, explaining to the congregation the arrangements which have been made. Those who do not participate should be instructed to wait quietly in the sanctuary for the conclusion of the service. The minister should then say:

Jesus said: "Ye call me Master and Lord: and ye say well; for so I am. If I then, your Lord and Master, have washed your feet; Ye also ought to wash one another's feet. For I have given you an example, that ye should do as I have done to you" (John 13:13-15).

This ordinance may be observed under the direction of the deacons and their wives. During its observance, the participants may share in a time of fellowship by singing and sharing testimonies. When the observance is concluded, the participants will again assemble in the sanctuary for the conclusion of the service. When everyone has reassembled, the minister should say:

"And when they had sung an hymn, they went out . . ." (Matthew 26:30). Let us sing hymn number ____________________.

At the close of the singing, the minister shall pronounce a blessing or closing prayer.

6
Dedication of Children I

Unless special circumstances prevent it,, this service should be held in the church. Arrangements for the dedication of a child should be made by the minister prior to the day of dedication. At that time the meaning of dedication and the parents' responsibility to bring up the child in the Christian faith should be clearly presented. At the proper time in the service the child will be presented to the minister by the parents.

Minister

The Holy Scriptures record for us that Elkanah and his wife brought their child to Eli, saying, "O my lord, as thy soul liveth, my lord, I am the woman that stood by thee here, praying unto the LORD. For this child I prayed; and the LORD hath given me my petition which I asked of him: therefore also I have lent him to the LORD; as long as he liveth he shall be lent to the LORD" (1 Samuel 1:26-28).

____________________________ (parents' name): In presenting your child for dedication to God, you express your love for (him/her), and your desire for the very best in (his/her) life. You desire that (he/she) may grow not only in strength and knowledge, but also in the fear and favor of God. With that in mind you must be careful to oversee every influence that may affect (his/her) youthful mind, and constantly encourage (him/her) to follow the Lord. And even more importantly, you must set an example for (him/her) by doing so yourselves.

Therefore, with your church family as witnesses, I challenge you in the presence of Almighty God, to constantly surround this child with every godly influence, and with your fervent prayers and unconditional love so that (he/she) may come to know God as Father, Jesus Christ as Savior, and the Holy Spirit as guide.

Knowing from Deuteronomy 6 that God has given parents the primary responsibility for the spiritual training of their children, do each of you, as parents of this child, solemnly promise before God and these witnesses that you will, to the best of your ability, strive to raise this child in the nurture and admonition of the Lord; will you be careful in your own conduct to live as Christian believers and as wholesome examples to this child; will you constantly pray for (him/her), and seek to teach (him/her) to avoid all evil habits and influences, and to turn (his/her) mind to the Holy Scriptures and (his/her) feet to the house of God, seeking to lead (him/her) to Christ when you feel (he/she) understands the meaning of your efforts; and will you make use of all helps that God gives you through godly family and through the teaching and training ministries of your church?

Parents

We do solemnly promise.

Minister to Father

I challenge you as a father to build and defend the home into which this little one has come. With God's help, strive for it to be a home built firmly upon the teachings of Jesus Christ, the Son of God. Let nothing enter your home that will tend to destroy faith, confidence, and mutual love without which no home can endure. Let nothing enter your home that will injure the soul of this little child, or crowd out the Master who said: "Whosoever shall receive one of such children in my name receiveth me."

Minister to Mother

I challenge you as a mother to always live with purity of heart and purpose. If your child grows up to know God in a personal experience, it will be largely because you have awakened (his/her) latent faith, and because you have nurtured (him/her) in the things of God. It is from you, the greatest object of (his/her) affection, that (he/she) gets (his/her) first idea of God. As you bow with this little one at your knee, the sense of awe and reverence is awakened in (his/her) soul. From the purity of your life comes the idea that God is holy, and from the gentleness of your voice, the idea that God is love.

The minister may now place his hand on the child's head or take the child in his arms and say:

____________________, I dedicate you to God and to the service of His kingdom, in the name of the Father, and the Son, and the Holy Spirit. Amen.

The minister returns the child if appropriate.

Minister

And now, having presented your child in dedication to God, do you also desire to reaffirm your dedication to Christ and your desire to live exemplary lives, relying upon the grace of God to exalt Christ by setting a godly example?

Parents

We do.

Minister

Having heard these vows and sacred promises, as a minister of Christ, I joyously entrust your child to the gracious and loving care of God, our Heavenly Father.

Your child will not remember this day; therefore tell (him/her) soon and often about the promises and the prayers made today in (his/her) behalf.

Prayer of Dedication

O Lord, we ask You to bless this child, whom we dedicate to You and to Your service forever. Lead (him/her), we pray to an early understanding of Your ways, and to a perfect trust in Christ, as Savior. Preserve and protect (him/her) from the dangers of life in this world, from the perils of doubt and the temptations of sin, and pour out on (him/her) the gift of Your grace that (he/she) may serve You with a faithful heart all the days of (his/her) life. And so we pray that You would protect and draw this family to You, that they may be united to Christ in faith and love and walk with You all the days of their lives. May they then stand together in Your presence around Your throne and worship You forever. Through Jesus Christ our Lord we pray. Amen.

7
Dedication of Children II

Unless special circumstances prevent it, this service should be held in the church. Arrangements for the dedication of a child should be made by the minister prior to the day of dedication. At that time the meaning of dedication and the parents' responsibility to bring up the child in the Christian faith should be clearly presented. At the proper time in the service the child will be presented to the minister by the parents.

Minister

My friends, this is a happy and significant occasion which brings us together. Like Mary and Hannah of old, you have brought your child to the house of God to present (him/her) to the Lord. You have heard the words of the Master, "Suffer little children, and forbid them not, to come unto me: for of such is the kingdom of heaven." The young life which you hold in your arms is both a mystery and a wonder. God has placed in your hearts a new and compelling sense of the dignity of life and the obligation of parenthood.

The Scriptures give us examples of how godly parents dedicated their children to the Lord and His service; Hannah brought her child, Samuel, and dedicated him to God and to the service of His house. Mary, the mother of

Jesus, brought the Child, according to the law of Moses, up to Jerusalem to present Him to the Lord.

We are confident, therefore, of God's divine approval as this child is brought this day to be dedicated to Him and His service. It is our duty as a Christian congregation to receive this child into the care of the church, and to minister to (him/her) in every way possible.

The Scriptures say, "Take heed that ye despise not one of these little ones; for I say unto you, that in heaven their angels do always behold the face of My Father which is in heaven. Even so it is not the will of your Father which is in heaven, that one of these little ones should perish."

"These words, which I command thee this day, shall be in thine heart: and thou shalt teach them diligently unto thy children, and shalt talk of them when thou sittest in thine house, and when thou walkest by the way, and when thou liest down, and when thou risest up."

"Train up a child in the way he should go: and when he is old, he will not depart from it."

God has a purpose for your child's life. To find that purpose and to live it out fully will mean blessing: to refuse or ignore it will mean failure. It is your privilege and duty to guide your child in such a way as to make the will of God the greatest ambition of (his/her) life.

To this task you are called to dedicate yourselves today; to this end you dedicate your child to God.

In accordance with the purpose for which you have come, will you please now respond to the following covenant?

Minister

Do you dedicate yourselves as parents to raise your child in the nurture and admonition of the Lord?

Parents

We do.

Minister

Do you promise to instruct (him/her) in the Bible and in the practice of prayer; to guide (him/her) in the development of a Christ-like character; and to diligently bring (him/her) to the services of the church where (he/she) will be taught the ways of the Lord?

Parents

We do.

Minister

Do you promise to try to the best of your ability to shape the home life of your child, by family devotions, and by your words and your example, so that (he/she) will come to receive and confess Christ when old enough to understand, and come into the fellowship and service of the church?

Parents

We do.

The minister may now place his hand on the child's head or take the child in his arms and say:

_____________, I dedicate you to God and to the service of His kingdom, in the name of the Father, and the Son, and the Holy Spirit. Amen.

If appropriate, the minister returns the child to a parent and may then, if he desires, present a New Testament.

Minister

In recognition of the dedication of your child, I present to you this New Testament inscribed with your child's name. From its pages I challenge you to instruct (him/her) in the way of life.

The minister will now ask the congregation to rise for the prayer of dedication.

Prayer of Dedication

The prayer should include requests for blessing and protection for the child and grace, wisdom and strength for the parents that they may bring up the child in the nurture and admonition of the Lord.

Benediction

The Lord bless you, and keep you; the Lord make His face shine upon you, and be gracious unto you; the Lord lift up His countenance upon you, and give you peace. Amen.

8

Dedication of Children III

Every child receives life from God. It is proper to recognize the sacredness of birth and life in a public worship service. In this service the child is presented before the Lord and the congregation. At the same time, the Christian parents publicly acknowledge their desire and obligation to raise their child to follow Christ.

Minister

We are gathered today in order that this child born to ____________________ and ____________________ may be presented before the Lord and this congregation. We rejoice with them in welcoming this new and precious life, which has come from our Heavenly Father, who breathes into all the breath of life, so that each person is created an immortal soul.

These parents have brought their child before their church family to acknowledge that this child is given to them as a gift and sacred trust from God.

Since the Scriptures teach the importance of obedience and guidance within the Christian family, we are certain of God's approval upon this act of dedication. In Ephesians 6:1-4 the apostle Paul gives this advice: "Children, obey your parents in the Lord; for this is right. Honour thy father and mother; which is the first commandment with promise; That it may be well with thee, and thou mayest live long on the earth. And ye fathers, provoke not your children to wrath; but bring them up in the nurture and admonition of the Lord."

Minister to Parents

As parents, you have been entrusted with a new life given by God. According to Deuteronomy 6, it is your duty to lead this child to know and love God, and, working in obedience to God's will, to help in the unfolding of (his/her) spiritual life. From your example the child must learn to pray. From your example (he/she) must learn to read and love the Bible, and from your example (he/she) must learn to walk in a daily relationship with Christ.

Above all you are to make it your constant prayer and desire that when (he/she) comes to the age of understanding (he/she) will choose of (his/her) own free will to accept and confess Christ as (his/her) Savior, to obey Him as Lord, and to give (himself/herself) in loyal and loving service as a member of the church, which is the Body of Christ.

Do you, ________________ and ________________, accept the awesome and serious responsibility with which God has entrusted you in the life of this child? If so, answer: WE DO.

Do you promise to pray for and with ________________ for (his/her) growth in knowledge of God, and in spiritual truth? If so, answer: WE DO.

Do you promise to train your child in body, mind, and soul for service to and fellowship with God and His Church? If so, answer: WE DO.

Do you promise to do all you can to lead (him/her) at an early age to confess (his/her) personal faith in Jesus Christ? If so, answer: WE DO.

The minister may now place his hand on the child's head or take the child in his arms and say:

Based on the confession your loving parents made today before God and this assembled body of believers, I now, with great joy, dedicate you, ____________________, to God in the name of the Father, Son, and the Holy Spirit. Amen.

Presentation of Child to the Congregation

Now, to the members of this congregation, I present this child ____________________ and (his/her) parents, ____________________. You, too, will have a part in the development of their growth as a family. You are needed to provide prayer support, assist in Bible teaching, share in fellowship, provide opportunities, facilities, and personnel through which these parents and this child may enter into the fullness of the Christian life and experience.

Do you promise to do all in your power to assist these parents in showing their child true godliness by living lives which model the Christian spirit? Do you promise to provide opportunities and facilities for training and growth in the Christian life? And do you promise to assist the parents in every way to bring this child to the place where (he/she) will choose Christ as (his/her) personal Savior and Lord at an early age? If so, answer: WE DO.

Prayer of Dedication

Our Father in Heaven, we give You our heartfelt thanks for the coming of this child into the world and into the life of this congregation. We acknowledge Your Lordship over all creation and accept this new life as a trust from You, the giver of all life.

We praise You for the love of these parents through whom You have created a new life. We thank You that under the ministry of Your Spirit they have been led to present their child to You in this public service.

We pray that Your divine blessings may rest upon these parents and this child. Grant these parents wisdom and power, love and compassion, tenderness and firmness as, together, they strive to fulfill the vows made this day before You and this congregation. Fill them with heavenly power as they undertake the task of leading their child to seek Christ. May they be privileged to see the fruit of their efforts as their child makes a personal commitment to Christ at an early age.

Let Your blessings rest upon this child, Father, we pray. And may the Holy Spirit guide (him/her) in the path of truth, lead (him/her) to accept Christ by faith, give (him/her) victory over evil, empower (him/her) to do Your service and live in holiness until You, at last, receive (him/her) into Your eternal home.

The Lord bless you and keep you;

The Lord make his face to shine upon you, and be gracious unto you;

The Lord lift up his countenance upon you, and give you peace. Amen.

9
Ordination of Ministers

When the appointed time for the ordination has arrived, the candidate having satisfied all requirements of the Ordaining Council, the Chairman will state the purpose of the meeting and make any remarks that may be appropriate to the occasion.

Hymn

Prayer

Scripture

How beautiful upon the mountains are the feet of him that bringeth good tidings, that publisheth peace; that bringeth good tidings of good, that publisheth salvation; that saith unto Zion, Thy God reigneth! Thy watchmen shall lift up the voice; with the voice together shall they sing: for they shall see eye to eye, when the LORD shall bring again Zion.

—Isaiah 52:7-8

Again the word of the LORD came unto me, saying, Son of man, speak to the children of thy people, and say unto them, When I bring the sword upon a land, if the people of the land take a man of their coasts, and set him for their watchman: If when he seeth the sword come upon the land, he blow the trumpet, and warn the people; Then whosoever heareth the sound of the trumpet, and taketh not warning; if the sword come, and take him away, his blood shall be upon his own head. He heard the sound of the trumpet, and took not warning; his blood shall be upon him. But he that taketh warning shall deliver his soul. But if the watchman see the sword come, and blow not the trumpet, and the people be not warned; if the sword come, and take any person from among them, he is taken away in his iniquity; but his blood will I require at the watchman's hand. So thou, O son of man, I have set thee a watchman unto the house of Israel; therefore thou shalt hear the word at my mouth, and warn them from me. When I say unto the wicked, O wicked man, thou shall surely die; if thou dost not speak to warn the wicked from his way, that wicked man shall die in his iniquity; but his blood will I require at thine hand. Nevertheless, if thou warn the wicked of his way to turn from it; if he do not turn from his way, he shall die in his iniquity; but thou hast delivered thy soul.

—Ezekiel 33:1-9

Now the Spirit speaketh expressly, that in the latter times some shall depart from the faith, giving heed to seducing spirits, and doctrines of devils; Speaking lies in hypocrisy; having their conscience seared with a hot iron; Forbidding to marry, and commanding to abstain from meats, which God hath created to be received with thanksgiving of them which believe and know the truth. For every creature of God is good, and nothing to be refused, if it be received with thanksgiving. For it is sanctified by the word of God and prayer. If thou put the brethren in remembrance of these things, thou shalt be a good minister of Jesus Christ, nourished up in the words of faith and of good doctrine, whereunto thou hast attained. But refuse profane and old wives' fables, and exercise thyself rather unto godliness. For bodily exercise profiteth little: but godliness is profitable unto all things, having promise of the life that now is, and of that which is to come. This is a faithful saying and worthy of all acceptation. For therefore we both labour and suffer reproach, because we trust in the living God, who is the Saviour of all men, specially of those that believe. These things command and teach. Let no man despise thy youth; but be thou an example of the believers, in word, in conversation, in charity, in spirit, in faith, in purity. Till I come, give attendance to reading, to exhortation, to doctrine. Neglect not the gift that is in thee, which was given thee by prophecy, with the laying on of the hands of the presbytery. Meditate upon these things; give thyself wholly to them; that thy profiting may appear to all. Take heed unto thyself, and unto the doctrine; continue in them: for in doing this thou shalt both save thyself, and them that hear thee.

—1 Timothy 4

The Chairman of the Ordaining Council may now ask the following questions:

Question

My brother, you are fully aware of the responsibilities that are about to be placed upon you by being ordained and set apart as an ambassador of Jesus Christ; therefore, with this knowledge, are you ready and willing to assume the responsibility?

Answer

I am, God being my Helper.

Question

Do you accept the Bible as the inspired and infallible Word of God?

Answer

I do, in all sincerity.

Question

Will you assume the responsibility to preach and teach God's Word with all love and boldness; to minister to the needs of those to whom you are sent without partiality; and to give of yourself sacrificially and without reserve to the building of the body of Christ?

Answer

I will, God being my Helper.

Question

Will you strive to be diligent in the study of God's Word; always ready and faithful in prayer; an example of Christian godliness and discipline before your people and the community, in order that your life may be a worthy Christian example and that the blessing of God may rest upon your ministry?

Answer

I will, God being my Helper.

Question

Recognizing the sacred responsibility of your call and aware of your own human weakness, will you seek to be directed and empowered by the Holy Spirit in order that you may be a faithful minister of Him who has called you?

Answer

I will, God being my Helper.

Prayer of Ordination

The candidate will kneel and be joined by all ordained ministers present who will place their hands upon him. The Prayer of Ordination is offered by someone previously selected.

*The Charge**

By a minister selected for the occasion.

Hymn

Benediction

*See section titled "Challenge to Minister."

10

Challenge to Minister I

In our challenge to you as a minister of the Lord Jesus Christ, let us hear first the word of God as spoken in the instruction of the apostle Paul to his son in the faith, Timothy:

"I charge thee, therefore, before God, and the Lord Jesus Christ, who shall judge the quick and the dead at his appearing and his kingdom; Preach the word; be instant in season, out of season; reprove, rebuke, exhort with all longsuffering and doctrine."

"Let no man despise thy youth; but be thou an example of the believers, in word, in conversation, in charity, in spirit, in faith, in purity."

"Give attendance to reading, to exhortation, to doctrine. Neglect not the gift that is in thee, which was given thee by prophecy, with the laying on the hands of the presbytery. Meditate upon these things, give thyself wholly to them; that thy profiting may appear to all. Take heed unto thyself, and unto the doctrine; continue thou in the things which thou hast learned and hast been assured of knowing of whom thou hast learned them; And that from a child thou hast known the Holy Scriptures, which are able to make thee wise unto salvation through faith which is in Christ Jesus."

"All scripture is given by inspiration of God, and is profitable for doctrine, for reproof, for correction, for instruction in righteousness; That the man of God may be perfect thoroughly furnished unto all good works."

My brother, as a minister you must never forget that if you have been called of God to preach, you are called to the highest and most noble calling in the world and you should approach it with such holy awe as to never do anything to dishonor your Lord or the sanctity of your profession.

You should always remember that you are set apart by God for the specific work of preaching the Gospel. You are given truth by God which you must reverently impart to man. You deal with God in behalf of men; you deal with men in behalf of God. Since as a minister you are God's ambassador to man, you should represent the things of God in your daily walk and conduct. Your life should be beyond reproach.

Always remember that you are to be a leader of men. This will call you to be an example of promptness, a student of humanity knowing how to deal with men, a preacher of scriptural sermons which are God-anointed, denouncing sin in the proper place and manner, but with the gift of discernment and love.

When dealing with delicate situations, don't speak until your statements have been well thought out. Think ahead. If a mistake is made, be Christian enough to acknowledge it. Your preaching will only be effective if you practice the truth in your daily life.

Finally, my brother, be spirit controlled. Be disciplined in every situation. Don't be a castaway. Be an overcomer, not one who gives in to temptation. Follow the advice of the apostle Paul: "But, I keep under my body and bring it into subjection, lest after I have preached to others, I myself also be a castaway."

As a minister, you should always feel that the world is your mission field, and that the church you serve is the organized force to work this large field. To do the most effective work, you should be a person of staunch loyalty to the church that is ordaining you and under whose blessing you serve, and yet empty of religious bigotry, being able to show the proper friendliness and cooperation with other denominations and fellowships without surrendering the distinctive scriptural truths you are called upon to teach and preach.

Your work will always be one of evangelism, always pursuing lost souls with a zeal which knows no rest, skillfully handling each one as the circumstances of each case may require. While it is true that your duties may involve primarily the responsibility of enlisting new recruits into the greater body of Christ, your confident faith in the doctrines and practices you sponsor should cause you to feel that saved people can serve God better by uniting with your church than anywhere else. If the doctrines of God's Word are to be passed along to the next generation, you will recognize there must be a continuing membership to do it.

"I give thee charge in the sight of God, who quickeneth all things, and before Christ Jesus, who before Pontius Pilate witnessed a good confession: That thou keep this commandment without spot, unrebukeable, until the appearing of our Lord Jesus Christ . . . Grace be with thee. Amen"

11

Challenge to Minister II

I would challenge you first, my brother, to always make your own faith and spiritual life your top priority. In the words of Paul to Timothy: "A bishop (the overseer of souls) then must be blameless, vigilant, sober, of good behavior, given to hospitality . . . not given to wine, no striker, not greedy of filthy lucre; but patient, not a brawler, not covetous . . . not a novice, lest being lifted up with pride he fall into condemnation of the devil. Moreover he must have a good report of them which are without."

The sermon preached by the life of the preacher carries far more weight than do those preached from the pulpit—so, let your life be an example. As Jude says: "Keep yourself in the love of God" and see to it that you live your life in a way that will glorify Him who has purchased you by His own blood, and will cause those around you to be challenged to glorify your heavenly Father with their lives also.

I further challenge you, my brother, with the fact that you are called to be a preacher. This statement on the surface may seem obvious. Do not be like many that have assumed the high calling of the ministry, and yet apparently are content to do very little about it, or have allowed it to become a "side-line." I feel it necessary to challenge you that if you are called to be a preacher, you must give it adequate time and priority.

You are not entering a profession. You are entering the work of a calling—a divine calling. Literally, you have not chosen, but have been chosen.

You are not out to make a living, but to make a life.

You are not out to *get,* but to *give.*

I challenge you, my brother, that the compelling motive that has stirred your very soul—that irresistible *call*, is the call to preach the Gospel. I challenge you, never step down to a lower task.

I further challenge you, my brother, that you are called to be a preacher of the Gospel of Jesus Christ.

Here I would remind you that if your living is provided through the ministry of your church, honesty demands that you preach with conviction the doctrines of that church—not with bigotry and hatred, but with Christian kindness and courtesy to all who may disagree.

However, with all the passion of my soul, I challenge you, my brother, preach the Gospel—not essays on moral subjects; not lectures on academic subjects; not theories—leave all these to those who do the lesser tasks. Remember, you are a preacher of the Gospel of Jesus Christ.

Even then, I challenge you, do not let your preaching be about Christ as the idealist, or as Christ the Great Teacher, or as Christ the perfect man— He is all of these and infinitely more. Preach the Gospel of Christ which is the power of God for salvation. Preach Him as the crucified, yet risen and ascended Christ of Calvary; the only hope, yet the sufficient hope of all men who will believe. I challenge you, my brother, preach the Gospel.

I would further remind you, my brother, of the serious responsibility of your calling.

1. The preacher of the Gospel does not deal with material things; but with eternal things.
2. He is responsible for the general spread of the Gospel.
3. He is responsible for the building up of the Christians over whom the Holy Spirit makes him the overseer. "Reprove, rebuke, and exhort with all longsuffering."
4. He is responsible for the unsaved of his congregation and community, and for all men who come under his ministry.

I challenge you to remember that God has set you as a watchman upon the wall. If you are unfaithful and do not warn the sinner with all your energy, God will hold you accountable.

I further remind you, my brother, of the sorrows and joys of your calling.

I would not be true to you, or to the high calling to which you come, if I were not to remind you that there will be sorrows—when those you trust betray you; when all the rage of hell seems to be directed against your soul; when failure comes after having done your best; when you must walk alone in order to be true to your convictions and the calling you have answered. Yes, there will be sorrows, but there are also *joys!*

Joy when victory comes at the end of each of the above named sorrows. Joy when you lighten someone's burden. Joy when you have brought sunlight into the shadows of someone's life. Unspeakable joy, my brother, when you have taken the hand of a lost sinner and placed it within the gasp of the nail-scarred hand of Jesus.

In the words of the apostle Paul to Timothy, his son in the ministry: "I charge thee before God, and the Lord Jesus Christ, who shall judge the quick and the dead at his appearing and his kingdom; preach the word; be instant in season, out of season; reprove, rebuke, exhort with all longsuffering and doctrine. For the time will come when they will not endure sound doctrine; but after their own lusts shall heap to themselves teachers, having itching ears; and they shall turn away their ears from the truth, and shall be turned into fables. But watch thou in all things, endure afflictions, do the work of an evangelist, make full proof of thy ministry."

And these next three verses remind you of the glorious end of your calling:

"For I am now ready to be offered, and the time of my departure is at hand. I have fought a good fight, I have finished my course, I have kept the faith: henceforth there is laid up for me a crown of righteousness, which the Lord, the righteous judge, shall give me at that day: and not to me only, but unto all them also that love his appearing."

The Lord bless you, and keep you; the Lord make his face to shine upon you, and be gracious unto you; the Lord lift up his countenance upon you, and give you peace. And may the God of peace, that brought again from the dead our Lord Jesus, that great Shepherd of the sheep, through the blood of the everlasting covenant, make you perfect in every good work to do His will, working in you that which is well pleasing in His sight, through Jesus Christ; to whom be glory for ever and ever. Amen.

God bless you, my brother.

*This challenge was adapted from the charge given to the author by his father.

12
Ordination of Deacons

The ordination service for a deacon may be a part of any duly called public service of the congregation at the discretion of the minister who will officiate at the service.

Opening Remarks

Our Lord's concern for man's physical and spiritual needs was evident in His ministry. He healed the sick. He fed the hungry. He restored sight to the blind. Early in the life of the Church she shared the concern of her Lord for this area of life and chose deacons to minister to people's needs. A long and honorable succession of deacons have expressed the conscience and concern of the Church for her people.

It is our privilege and responsibility as followers of Christ to share His concern for those within the Church and those without. The deacon becomes the heart and hand of the Church in seeking out and ministering to their need. In this area the deacon is the conscience of the congregation; the right hand of the pastor.

Deacons were first appointed in the church at Jerusalem, and an account of their appointment is given in the sixth chapter of the Acts of the Apostles as follows:

And in those days, when the number of the disciples was multiplied, there arose a murmuring of the Grecians against the Hebrews, because their widows were neglected in the daily ministration. Then the twelve called the multitude of the disciples unto them, and said, It is not reason that we should leave the word of God, and serve tables. Wherefore, brethren, look ye out among you seven men of honest report, full of the Holy Ghost and wisdom, whom we may appoint over this business. But we will give ourselves continually to prayer, and to the ministry of the word. And the saying pleased the whole multitude: and they chose Stephen, a man full of faith and of the Holy Ghost, and Philip, and Prochorus, and Nicanor, and Timon, and Parmenas, and Nicolas a proselyte of Antioch: Whom they set before the apostles: and when they had prayed, they laid their hands on them.

—Acts 6:1-6

Following this precedent established by the first Christian Church, the brothers and sisters of this congregation have chosen from among themselves men with good reputations and full of the Holy Spirit and wisdom, to serve as deacons. We are gathered to formally install our brother(s) to this office. Let us pray.

Prayer

The deacon or deacons to be ordained should now come forward and stand before the minister.

Since you have been elected to the office of deacon in this church, and have declared your willingness to serve,

I now ask you to affirm that by answering the following questions:

Question

Do you reaffirm your allegiance to Jesus Christ and His Church?

Response

I do.

Question

Do you accept the office of deacon in this church, and promise to faithfully perform its duties?

Response

I do, the Lord being my Helper.

Question

Do you promise to further the interests of the church to the best of your ability, and to cooperate with the pastor and members in promoting the harmonious and effective working of all its ministries?

Response

I do, the Lord being my Helper.

The minister will now address the congregation.

Do you, the members of this church, acknowledge and receive this brother as your deacon? Do you promise to give to him that esteem, encouragement, and cooperation of which this office is worthy? If so, will you signify this by standing and uniting your hearts in the prayer of ordination. Let us pray.

Prayer of Ordination

> *The candidate will kneel and the minister, with hands resting on his head, will offer prayer in his own words, or the following:*

O Lord Jesus, who did not come to be ministered to, but to minister, and who is the Head of the Church, set apart and consecrate this Your servant to the office of deacon. Fill him with heavenly wisdom, that in counsel he may deal wisely as those who have the mind of Christ. Give him the spirit of compassion for human needs, and fill him with love and tender care for every soul for whom You have died. Strengthen and nourish his faith in You and in the values of Your Church, that he may increase the faith of his fellow members. And give grace to us all, that working together, seeking to know and do Your will, we may greatly advance your cause in this community; to the glory of Your name. Amen.

Charge

By virtue of your call to the office of deacon by this congregation, and your satisfactory fulfillment of the requirements for deacon as found in God's Holy Word, I do now install you as deacon of the ____________________ congregation for the term of service to which you have been called.

This charge is to be repeated if more than one deacon is installed.

Benediction

May God bless you in these responsibilities and make you fruitful in all your service. May you be a faithful steward over these few things, that in the end you may be made ruler over many things. And may the Church prosper and Jesus be honored by your faithfulness. Amen.

13

Installation Service for Officers and Teachers

This order of installation may be used during a regular Sunday morning worship service or some other appropriate time.

Hymn

As the hymn is being sung, the leaders and teachers will come before the minister, after which the minister will address them in his own words or the following:

Friends and fellow workers: In calling you to be teachers and officers in it's educational ministries, the church has committed to you as important a task as lies within her power to give. Yours is the high privilege of guiding and inspiring boys and girls, men and women in the ways of the Lord. In this you are co-laborers with Jesus Christ, the great Teacher, and join the noble succession of loyal and patient souls who have carried the light of the Gospel forward from one generation to another. By your words and by your example you will be constantly influencing those entrusted to your care in the most important things of life: the seeking of God and His will, and the dedication of their hearts to His service.

I challenge you, therefore, to be faithful, dedicated, sympathetic, and persevering, always keeping in mind that the great goal of Christian education and training is not merely the imparting of information, but the awakening and inspiring of the soul; that as Jesus increased in wisdom and stature and in favor with God and man, so your pupils may grow in grace and in the knowledge of the truth.

Covenant of Teachers and Officers

Having been called to the ministry of teaching and training in this church, will you strive, with God as your helper, to faithfully perform your duties? Will you work hard to study and prepare, be regular and punctual in attendance at church and your class; and will you maintain a sympathetic and friendly relationship with your pupils, diligently seeking by word and example to win them to Jesus Christ and the Church?

Teachers and Officers

We will.

Pledge of Church Membership

The minister may then call upon the members of the Church to stand, and may address them as follows:

Members of our Church, you have witnessed the pledges of these leaders and teachers. Will you show your appreciation of their efforts by determining to do your part, to be regular in attendance, attentive and involved during class, and loyal to the Master whom we serve?

Response

We will.

Prayer of Consecration

In the minister's own words or the following:

Eternal God our Father, who has called us into Your service and who has promised grace and strength for the fulfilling of Your will: Look favorably upon these Your servants who now dedicate themselves to their task in this church. Give them wisdom and insight that they may see the potential in the lives of those they teach, and never grow weary in their efforts to win them to Christ. Fill them with Your Spirit, and grant that they may realize that in all their efforts You are their Companion, their Leader, and their Friend. Give to those who teach and to those who are taught the spirit of understanding and obedience. May they increase in wisdom and stature, and in favor with God and man. In the name of our Lord and Master, we pray. Amen.

Hymn

Benediction

Now unto Him that is able to do exceeding abundantly above all that we ask or think, according to the power that worketh in us, unto Him be glory in the Church by Christ Jesus throughout all ages, world without end. And may the love of God, and the grace of Jesus Christ, and the comfort of the Holy Spirit be with you all. Amen.

14
Marriage Ceremony I

At the day and time appointed for the wedding ceremony, the persons to be married will take their places before the minister, and in the sight of those witnessing the ceremony. With the man on the left hand, and the woman on the right, the minister shall say:

Dearly beloved, we are gathered together here in the sight of God to join together this man and this woman in holy marriage, which is an honorable institution, established by God, symbolizing for us the mystical union that is between Christ and His church: which holy practice Christ adorned and beautified with His presence and first miracle that He performed in Cana of Galilee, and is commended by Saint Paul to be honorable among all men: and therefore is not to be entered into unadvisedly or lightly; but reverently, discreetly, advisedly, soberly, and in the fear of God. Into this holy union these two persons come now to be joined. If any man can show just cause, why they may not lawfully be joined together, let him speak now, or forever hold his peace.

And also speaking to the persons who are to be married, he shall say:

I require and charge you both before God, that if either of you know any reason why you may not be lawfully joined together in marriage, you must now confess it. For be assured that if any persons are joined together in a way other than as God's Word allows, their marriage is not lawful.

The minister, if he should have any reason to doubt the lawfulness of the proposed marriage, may demand sufficient assurance for his protection; but if no obstacle shall be alleged or suspected, the minister shall say to the man:

____________________, will you have this woman to be your wedded wife, to live together after God's ordinance in the holy union of marriage? Will you love her, honor, and keep her in sickness and in health; and forsaking all others, keep yourself only for her, so long as you both shall live?

The man shall answer:

I will.

Then shall the minister say to the woman:

____________________, will you have this man to be your wedded husband, to live together after God's ordinance in the holy union of marriage? Will you love him, comfort him, honor, and keep him in sickness and in health; and, forsaking all others, keep yourself only for him, so long as you both shall live?

The woman shall answer:

I will.

Then the minister shall say:

Who gives this woman to be married to this man?

Then they will give their pledge to each other in this manner. The minister, receiving the woman at her father's or friend's hands, shall ask the man with his right hand to take the woman by her right hand, and to repeat after him as follows:

I, ____________________ , take you, __________________ , to be my wedded wife, to have and to hold from this day forward, for better, for worse, for richer, for poorer, in sickness and in health, to love and to cherish, till death us do part, according to God's holy ordinance.

Then the woman shall also repeat after the minister:

I, ____________________ , take you, __________________ , to be my wedded husband, to have and to hold from this day forward, for better, for worse, for richer, for poorer, in sickness and in health, to love and to cherish, till death us do part, according to God's holy ordinance.

And before delivering the ring to the man, the minister may say as follows:

Bless, O Lord, this ring, that he who gives it and she who wears it may abide in Your peace, and continue in Your favor, till their life's end; through Jesus Christ our Lord. Amen.

Then the man shall give a ring to the woman as follows: the minister shall give the ring to the man to put it on the third finger of the woman's left hand. And the man holding the ring there, and repeating after the minister, shall say:

With this ring I wed you in the name of the Father, and of the Son, and of the Holy Spirit. Amen.

If the man is also receiving a ring, the woman shall place the ring on the man's hand as above and shall repeat the following:

With this ring I wed you in the name of the Father, and of the Son, and of the Holy Spirit. Amen.

Let us pray.

Then the minister shall ask the people to stand and pray the Lord's Prayer.

Our Father, who art in Heaven, Hallowed be thy name. Thy kingdom come. Thy will be done, on earth as it is in Heaven. Give us this day our daily bread. And forgive us our trespasses as we forgive those who trespass against us. And lead us not into temptation, but deliver us from evil. For thine is the kingdom, and the power, and the glory, for ever and ever. Amen.

Then shall the minister add:

O eternal God, creator, and preserver of all mankind, giver of all spiritual grace, the author of everlasting life; send Your blessing upon these Your servants, this man and this woman, whom we bless in Your name; that they, living faithfully together, may perform and keep the vows and covenant they have made (of which this ring given and received is a token and pledge), and may always remain in perfect love and peace together, and live according to Your laws; through Jesus Christ our Lord, Amen.

Then shall the minister join their right hands together and say:

Those whom God has joined together, let no man put apart.

Then shall the minister speak to the witnesses.

Since ____________________ and ____________________ have chosen to join together in holy marriage, and have witnessed the same before God and this company, and have given and pledged their faithfulness, to each other, and have declared the same by giving and receiving a ring, and by joining hands; I pronounce that they are man and wife, in the name of the Father, and of the Son, and of the Holy Spirit. Amen.

The man and wife kneeling, the minister shall add this blessing:

May God the Father, God the Son, and God the Holy Spirit, bless, preserve, and keep you; and the Lord look upon you with mercy and favor, and fill you with all spiritual blessing and grace; that you may live together in this life in such a way that in the world to come you may have life everlasting. Amen.

15
Marriage Ceremony II

At the time appointed, the persons to be married—having been qualified according to the law of the state and the standards of the church—shall stand together facing the minister, the man at the minister's left hand and the woman at the right, the minister shall say:

Dear family and friends, we are gathered here in the sight of God, and in the presence of these witnesses, to join together this man and this woman in holy marriage; which is an honorable institution, established by God, and symbolizing for us the mystical union which exists between Christ and His Church; which holy practice Christ endorsed with His presence in Cana of Galilee. It is therefore not to be entered into unadvisedly, but reverently, discreetly, and in the fear of God. Into this holy union these two persons come now to be joined.

Speaking to the persons to be married, the minister shall say:

I require and challenge you both, as you stand in the presence of God, to remember that love and loyalty alone will stand as the foundation of a happy and enduring home. No other human ties are more tender, no other promises more sacred than those you make today. If you faithfully keep these promises, and if you constantly seek to do the will of your heavenly Father, your life will be full of joy, and the home which you are establishing will be at peace.

Then shall the minister say to the man, using his Christian name:

____________________, will you have this woman to be your wife, to live together in the holy union of marriage? Will you love her, comfort her, honor and keep her in sickness and in health; and forsaking all others keep yourself only for her, as long as you both shall live?

The man shall answer:

I will.

Then shall the minister say to the woman, using her Christian name:

____________________, will you have this man to be your husband, to live together in the holy union of marriage? Will you love him, comfort him, honor and keep him, in sickness and in health: and forsaking all others keep yourself only for him, as long as you both shall live?

The woman shall answer:

I will.

Then may the minister say:

Who gives this woman to be married to this man?

The father of the woman, or whoever gives her in marriage, shall answer:

I do.

Then the minister (receiving the hand of the woman from her father or other sponsor) shall ask the man with his right hand to take the woman by her right hand, and say after him:

I ________________ , take you, ________________ , to be my wife, to have and to hold, from this day forward, for better, for worse, for richer, for poorer, in sickness and in health, to love and to cherish, till death parts us, according to God's holy ordinance; and before God I pledge you my faithfulness.

Then shall they loose their hands; and the woman, with her right hand taking the man by his right hand, shall say after the minister:

I ________________ , take you, ________________ , to be my husband, to have and to hold, from this day forward, for better, for worse, for richer, for poorer, in sickness and in health, to love and to cherish, till death parts us, according to God's holy ordinance; and before God I pledge you my faithfulness.

Then shall they again loose their hands, and the man may give to the woman a ring, as follows: the minister, taking the ring, shall say:

This ring is an outward and visible symbol of an inward and spiritual commitment, signifying to all the uniting of this man and this woman in holy marriage, through Jesus Christ our Lord.

Then the minister may say:

Let us pray.

Bless, O Lord, the giving of this ring, that he who gives it and she who wears it may remain always in Your peace, and continue in Your favor; through Jesus Christ our Lord. Amen.

The minister shall then give the ring to the man to put upon the third finger of the woman's left hand. The man, holding the ring there, shall say after the minister:

As a symbol and pledge of the vows we have made, with this ring I marry you, in the name of the Father, and of the Son, and of the Holy Spirit. Amen.

The above portion of the ceremony should be repeated if the man is to receive a ring.

Then shall the minister say:

Let us pray.

O, eternal God, creator and preserver of all mankind, giver of all spiritual grace, the author of everlasting life; send Your blessing upon this man and this woman, whom we bless in Your name; that they may perform and keep the promises and covenant they have made, and may always remain together in perfect love and peace, and live according to Your laws.

Pour out Your grace on them, that they may love, honor, and cherish each other, and so live together in faithfulness and patience, in wisdom and true godliness, that their home may be a haven of blessing and a place of peace; through Jesus Christ our Lord. Amen.

Then shall the minister join their right hands together and with his hand on their united hands shall say:

Since ____________________ and ____________________ have chosen to join together in holy marriage, and have expressed that desire before God and these witnesses, and have pledged their faithfulness to each other, and have demonstrated it by joining hands and by giving and receiving a ring; I pronounce that they are husband and wife together, in the name of the Father, and of the Son, and of the Holy Spirit. Those whom God has joined together, let no man separate. Amen.

Then, the husband and wife kneeling, the minister shall say:

Let us pray.

Our Father who art in Heaven, hallowed be thy name; thy kingdom come; thy will be done on earth as it is in Heaven. Give us this day our daily bread. And forgive us our trespasses, as we forgive those who trespass against us. And lead us not into temptation, but deliver us from evil. For thine is the kingdom, and the power, and the glory, forever. Amen.

Then shall the minister add this blessing:

May God the Father, the Son, and the Holy Spirit, bless, preserve, and keep you; may the Lord graciously bless you with His favor, and so fill you with grace and love that you may live the rest of your lives together in joy and happiness. Amen.

16
Marriage Ceremony III

At the hour of the marriage, when the party is assembled before the minister, he shall say:

We are gathered together in the sight of God and these witnesses, to join together this man and this woman in holy matrimony. Marriage is the first institution given for the welfare of the human race. In the ancient Garden of Eden, before the tempter had touched the world, God saw that it was not good for the man to be alone. He made a helper suitable for him and established the practice of marriage, while heavenly hosts witnessed the wonderful scene.

Originated in divine wisdom and goodness, designed to promote human happiness and holiness, this union is the foundation of home life and social order, and so must remain till the end of time. It was sanctioned and honored by the presence and power of Jesus at the marriage in Cana of Galilee, and marked the beginning of His wondrous works. It was commended by Paul to be honorable among all men. Aside from receiving Christ as Savior and Lord, it is the most important step in life and, therefore, is not to be entered into unadvisedly or lightly, but reverently, discreetly, advisedly, and in the fear of God. Who gives this woman in marriage?

Then shall the father of the bride answer:

I do. (Or, Her mother and I do.)

The father of the bride, having given his daughter in marriage, shall take his seat by the bride's mother, and the minister shall continue:

From God's Word we read these words: From the beginning of the creation God made them male and female. And the LORD God said, It is not good that the man should be alone; I will make a helpmate for him. For this cause shall a man leave his father and mother, and cleave to his wife; And the two shall be one flesh: so then they are no more separate, but one flesh. Wives, submit yourselves unto your own husbands, as unto the Lord. For the husband is the head of the wife, even as Christ is the head of the church: and he is the Saviour of the body.

Therefore as the church is subject unto Christ, so let the wives be to their own husbands in every thing.

Husbands, love your wives, even as Christ also loved the church, and gave Himself for it.

So ought men to love their wives as their own bodies. He that loveth his wife loveth himself.

Nevertheless let every one of you in particular so love his wife even as himself; and the wife see that she reverence her husband.

You, ________________ , and you, ________________ , have come to me expressing your desire to be formally united in marriage, and being assured that no legal, moral, or religious barriers hinder this proper union, I ask you to join your right hands and give attention to the following questions.

Then the minister shall direct the following specifically to the groom:

____________________, in taking the woman whom you hold by the right hand to be your wife, I require you to promise to love and cherish her, to honor and sustain her, in sickness and in health, in poverty as in wealth, in the bad that may darken your days, in the good that may lighten your ways, and to be true to her in all things until death alone parts you.

Do you so promise?

Then shall the groom promise:

I do.

And the minister shall direct the following specifically to the bride:

____________________, in taking the man who holds you by the right hand to be your husband, I require you to promise to love and cherish him, to honor and sustain him, in sickness as in health, in poverty as in wealth, in the bad that may darken your days, in the good that may lighten your ways, and to be true to him in all things until death alone parts you.

Do you so promise?

Then shall the bride promise:

I do.

The minister then continues:

A new commandment I give unto you, That you love one another; as I have loved you, that you also love one another.

Love suffers long, and is kind; love envies not; love vaunts not itself, is not puffed up.

Does not behave itself unseemly, seeks not her own, is not easily provoked, thinks no evil; rejoices not in iniquity, but rejoices in the truth.

Bears all things, believes all things, hopes all things, endures all things.

Love never fails, for love is of God.

And now abides faith, hope, love, these three; but the greatest of these is love.

Then shall the minister take in his hand the ring for the bride and continue:

The ring is a symbol of the love you have for each other. Its unending circle represents the unchanging quality of your love and the gold represents the purity of that love. As a ceaseless reminder of this hour and as a seal of the promises you make, you will now give and receive your rings.

To the groom he will say:

Do you ______________ give this ring to ______________ as a token of your love for her?

The groom shall answer:

I do.

The minister shall then direct the groom to repeat after him:

I, ________________ , take you, ________________ , to be my wife, to have and to hold from this day forward, for better, for worse, for richer, for poorer, in sickness and in health, to love and to cherish, till death parts us, according to God's holy Word, and before God I pledge you my love.

Then shall the minister ask the bride:

Will you, ________________, take this ring as a token of ________________'s love for you, and will you wear it as a token of your love for him?

Then shall the bride promise:

I will.

Then the minister will say to the bride:

Do you, ____________, give this ring to ____________ as a token of your love for him?

And the bride shall promise:

I do.

The minister shall then direct the bride to repeat after him:

I, ________________ , take you, ________________ , to be my husband, to have and to hold, from this day forward, for better, for worse, for richer, for poorer, in sickness and in health, to love and to cherish, till death parts us, according to God's holy Word, and before God I pledge you my love.

The minister shall then ask the groom:

Will you, ____________________, take this ring as a token of ____________________'s love for you, and will you wear it as a token of your love for her?

The groom shall then promise:

I will.

The minister shall then lead in prayer. (Sometimes a wedding prayer is sung.) Then the minister continues:

You shalt love the Lord your God with all your heart, and with all your soul, and with all your might.

And these words, which I command you this day, shall be in your heart: And you shalt teach them diligently unto your children, and shall talk of them when you sit in your house.

Put on therefore, as the elect of God, kindness, humbleness of mind, meekness, longsuffering;

Forbearing one another, and forgiving one another.

And above all these things put on love, which is the bond of perfectness.

And let the peace of God rule in your hearts.

Having pledged your faith in, and love to each other, and having sealed your marital promises by giving and receiving the rings, acting in the authority vested in me by the laws of this state, and looking to heaven for divine sanction, I pronounce you husband and wife in the presence of God and these assembled witnesses.

What God has joined together, let no man separate.

And now may the God of peace prosper and bless you in this new relationship, and may the grace of Jesus Christ be yours in abundance now and forevermore.

17

Marriage Ceremony IV

Marriage is ancient and magnificent; it was first instituted by Almighty God, and given to man in a state of innocence and happiness.

"But from the beginning of creation God made them male and female. For this cause shall a man leave his father and his mother, and cleave to his wife; And they twain shall be one flesh" (Mark 10:6-8).

Friends and family, we now have the pleasure of seeing two of our friends present themselves here before God and these witnesses for the purpose of being united in the bonds of marriage, and we pray that God will pour out on them His blessings. Therefore, if any person can show just cause why they may not be lawfully joined together, let them now speak or forever hold their peace.

The minister shall then say:

____________________ , will you take the woman whom you hold by the hand to be your lawful wife—to love her, to honor and protect her, and forsaking all others to be loyal to her, and her alone, so long as you both shall live?

The man will answer:

I will.

The minister shall then say:

____________________, will you take the man whom you hold by the hand to be your lawful husband—to love him, to cherish him, to honor and obey him, and forsaking all others to be loyal to him, and him alone, so long as you both shall live?

The woman shall then say:

I will.

Minister

Now, upon your mutual promise, made in the presence of God and these witnesses, I pronounce you husband and wife, in the name of the Father, and of the Son and the Holy Spirit. May God bless you and keep you mindful of your promises and preserve you blameless, and may your lives be devoted to obedience to God's commands. Amen.

18
Marriage Ceremony V

Pastor: On behalf of **(Groom)** and **(Bride)**, I want to welcome all of you to this special occasion. I know that it means a great deal to them to have their family and friends here.

We've come together today in the sight of God to join together **(Groom)** and **(Bride)** in Christian marriage. This celebration is an outward symbol of a sacred and inward union of their hearts, a union which this couple freely chooses because of their love and commitment to each other.

Marriage is God's idea; it was instituted by Him, and when His purpose and design for marriage are followed, it provides the most intimate bond of love and fulfillment that can be experienced by two people on this earth.

In the Bible, God instructs husbands to love their wives in the same way that Christ loves His church, and gave Himself up for her. Wives are instructed to voluntarily place themselves under the loving leadership of their husband, just as the church submits to Christ's loving leadership. They are both instructed to make their marriage relationship the top priority, above all other relationships. They are to stick together like glue, and function as one unit. Husbands and wives, and all of us, are instructed to put each other's needs and interests ahead of our own. And this relationship should be a picture to all of the intimate relationship that Christ wants with his people.

(Groom) and **(Bride)**, you are responsible to God for your marriage.

I require and challenge you both, as you stand in the presence of God, to remember that unconditional love and commitment alone will stand as the foundation of a happy and lasting marriage. No other human ties are more tender, no other promises more sacred, than those you make today. If you keep these promises, and if you constantly seek to do what is best for one another, your life will be full of joy, and your home will be a place of peace and happiness.

(Groom), will you have this woman to be your wife, to live together in the holy union of marriage? Will you love her, comfort her, honor and keep her, in sickness and in health; and forsaking all others, keep yourself only for her, so long as you both shall live? If so, answer, "I will."

Groom: I will.

Pastor: **(Bride)**, will you have this man to be your husband, to live together in the holy union of marriage? Will you love him, comfort him, honor and keep him, in sickness and in health; and forsaking all others, keep yourself only for him so long as you both shall live? If so, answer, "I will."

Bride: I will.

Pastor: Please face each other in order to give your marriage vows. **(Groom)**, please repeat after me.

I, **(Groom)**, take you, **(Bride)**, / to be my wife--/ to have and to hold / from this day forward, / for better, for worse, / for richer, for poorer, / in sickness and health, / to love and to cherish, / till death do us part, / according to God's Holy Word, / and before God / I pledge you my loyalty.

(Bride), please repeat after me.

I, **(Bride)**, take you, **(Groom)**, / to be my husband-- / to have and to hold / from this day forward, / for better, for worse, / for richer, for poorer, / in sickness and health, / to love and to cherish, / till death do us part, / according to God's Holy Word, / and before God / I pledge you my loyalty.

Pastor: **(Groom)**, please hand me the ring.

Pastor: The wedding ring is an outward and visible symbol of an inward and spiritual commitment, signifying to all the uniting of this man and this woman in holy marriage, through Jesus Christ our Lord.

(Groom), do you give this ring to **(Bride)** as a symbol of your love for her?

Groom: I do.

Pastor: **(Bride)**, will you receive this ring as a symbol of **(Groom's)** love for you, and will you wear it as a symbol of your love for him?

Bride: I will.

[*Pastor gives the ring back to Groom.*]

Pastor: **(Groom)**, place the ring on **(Bride's)** finger and repeat after me.

In symbol and pledge / of the vows we have made/ with this ring / I marry you / in the name of the Father, / and of the Son, / and of the Holy Spirit./ Amen.

Pastor: **(Bride)**, please hand me the ring.

Pastor: **(Bride)**, do you give this ring to **(Groom)** as a symbol of your love for him?

Bride: I do.

Pastor: **(Groom)**, will you receive this ring as a symbol of **(Bride's)** love for you, and will you wear it as a symbol of your love for her?

Groom: I will.

[*Pastor gives the ring back to Bride.*]

Pastor: **(Bride)**, place the ring on **(Groom's)** finger and repeat after me.

In symbol and pledge / of the vows we have made / with this ring / I marry you / in the name of the Father, / and of the Son, / and of the Holy Spirit./ Amen.

Pastor: **(Groom)**, from this moment on you must dedicate yourself to be the loving leader of your family. Marriage is about serving, not being served. If you are to have the kind of marriage you have expressed the desire to have, you must choose every day to serve **(Bride)**, asking God's help to discern her needs and then to lay down your life to meet them. Unless you draw upon the grace of God every day, you will fail. Make it your aim each day to fulfill **(Bride's)** needs and the Lord will cause your relationship together to grow strong and rich.

(Bride), becoming **(Groom's)** wife means that you will now have the greatest influence on his life. No husband achieves his potential in life without the love, respect, and encouragement of his wife. You must seek God's help if you are to succeed in understanding and meeting **(Groom's)** needs.

Be his encourager; lift him up every day with your words and your actions.

A wedding doesn't make a marriage, it only begins one. A strong marriage is built with much attention and effort. You will be tempted in days to come to neglect each other's needs and to focus on your own. You will from time to time wonder what ever made you think you had anything in common. Satan will see to it that there is ample opportunity for you to question whether you've done the right thing, and whether it's worth the trouble to stay together.

When those times of turmoil and doubt come, as they do in every marriage, I charge you to remember the promises you have made today. Marriage is not a contract based on mutual satisfaction; it is a commitment to love and serve one another; it is a holy covenant sealed by the authority of God's eternal Word and the anointing of His Holy Spirit. With God's help you can realize the full potential of the home for which you dream and pray. It can be a haven of love, joy, peace, and fulfillment.

I challenge all of us who share this day with you to commit our prayers, encouragement, and guidance to help you succeed.

Let us join our hearts together in prayer for God's blessing on **(Groom)** and **(Bride)**.

[*Prayer*]

Pastor: You have chosen to illustrate the uniting of your lives in marriage through the lighting of a unity candle. Each of you will take the individual candle which represents your singleness and join the flames together to create a new flame which represents your union in marriage. As you blow out your individual candles, you are signifying the surrender of your singleness to the union of marriage. From this point on your lives are bound together. It is no longer "I, me, and mine," but "we, us, and ours."

[Lighting of the unity candle]

Since **(Groom)** and **(Bride)** have agreed together to join in holy marriage, and have pledged their love and faithfulness to each other, and have demonstrated this by joining hands and by giving and receiving rings, I pronounce that they are husband and wife together, in the name of the Father, and of the Son, and of the Holy Spirit. Those whom God has joined together, let no man tear apart.

(Groom), you may kiss your bride.

Ladies and gentlemen, it is my pleasure to present to you Mr. and Mrs. (Groom's name).

19
Visitation of the Sick

It is the duty and privilege of every pastor to visit the sick; to read to, pray for, and encourage those who are Christians and to try to bring those who are not Christians to Christ as Savior. Almost everyone will appreciate the reading of God's Word and prayer when sick. The wise pastor will not miss these opportunities to minister. Appropriate Scripture selections are suggested as follows:

Christians Who Are Sick

Let not your heart be troubled: ye believe in God, believe also in me. In my Father's house are many mansions: if it were not so, I would have told you. I go to prepare a place for you. And if I go and prepare a place for you, I will come again, and receive you unto myself; that where I am, there ye may be also. And whither I go ye know, and the way ye know. Thomas saith unto him, Lord, we know not whither thou goest; and how can we know the way? Jesus saith unto him, I am the way, the truth, and the life: no man cometh unto the Father, but by me. If ye had known me, ye should have known my Father also: and from henceforth ye know him, and have seen him. Philip saith unto him, Lord, shew us the Father, and it sufficeth us. Jesus saith unto him, Have I been so long time with you, and yet hast thou not known me, Philip? he that hath seen me hath seen the Father; and how sayest thou then, Shew us the Father? Believest thou not that I am in the Father, and the Father in me? the words that I speak unto you I speak not of myself: but the Father that dwelleth in me, he doeth the works. Believe me that I am in the Father, and the Father in me: or else believe me for the very works' sake. Verily, verily, I say unto you, He that believeth on me, the works that I do shall he do also; and greater works than these shall he do; because I go unto my Father. And whatsoever ye shall ask in my name, that will I do, that the Father may be glorified in the Son. If ye shall ask any thing in my name, I will do it. If ye love me, keep my commandments. And I will pray the Father, and he shall give you another Comforter, that he may abide with you for ever; Even the Spirit of truth; whom the world cannot receive, because it seeth him not, neither knoweth him: but ye know him; for he dwelleth with you, and shall be in you. I will not leave you comfortless: I will come to you. Yet a little while, and the world seeth me no more; but ye see me: because I live, ye shall live also. At that day ye shall know that I am in my Father, and ye in me, and I in you. He that hath my commandments, and keepeth them, he it is that loveth me: and he that loveth me shall be loved of my Father, and I will love him, and will manifest myself to him.

—John 14:1-21

These words spake Jesus, and lifted up his eyes to heaven, and said, Father, the hour is come; glorify thy Son, that thy Son also may glorify thee: As thou hast given him power over all flesh, that he should give eternal life to as many as thou hast given him. And this is life eternal, that they might know thee the only true God, and

Jesus Christ, whom thou hast sent. I have glorified thee on the earth: I have finished the work which thou gavest me to do. And now, O Father, glorify thou me with thine own self with the glory which I had with thee before the world was. I have manifested thy name unto the men which thou gavest me out of the world: thine they were, and thou gavest them me; and they have kept thy word. Now they have known that all things whatsoever thou hast given me are of thee. For I have given unto them the words which thou gavest me; and they have received them, and have known surely that I came out from thee, and they have believed that thou didst send me. I pray for them: I pray not for the world, but for them which thou hast given me; for they are thine. And all mine are thine, and thine are mine; and I am glorified in them. And now I am no more in the world, but these are in the world, and I come to thee. Holy Father, keep through thine own name those whom thou hast given me, that they may be one, as we are. While I was with them in the world, I kept them in thy name: those that thou gavest me I have kept, and none of them is lost, but the son of perdition; that the scripture might be fulfilled. And now come I to thee; and these things I speak in the world, that they might have my joy fulfilled in themselves. I have given them the word; and the world hath hated them, because they are not of the world, even as I am not of the world. I pray not that thou shouldest take them out of the world, but that thou shouldest keep them from the evil. They are not of the world, even as I am not of the world. Sanctify them through thy truth: thy word is truth. As thou hast sent me into the world, even so have I also sent them into the world. And for their sakes I sanctify myself, that they also might be sanctified through the truth. Neither pray I for these alone, but for them also which shall believe on me through their word; That they all may be one; as thou, Father, art in me, and I in thee, that they also may be one in us: that the world may believe that thou hast sent me. And the glory which thou gavest me I have given them; that they may be one, even as we are one: I in them, and thou in me, that they may be made perfect in one; and that the world may know that thou hast sent me, and hast loved them, as thou hast loved me.

—John 17:1-23

He that dwelleth in the secret place of the most High shall abide under the shadow of the Almighty. I will say of the LORD, He is my refuge and my fortress: my God; in him will I trust. Surely he shall deliver thee from the snare of the fowler, and from the noisome pestilence. He shall cover thee with his feathers, and under his wings shalt thou trust: his truth shall be thy shield and buckler.

—Psalm 91:1-4

For we know that if our earthly house of this tabernacle were dissolved, we have a building of God, an house not made with hands, eternal in the heavens. For in this we groan, earnestly desiring to be clothed upon with our house which is from heaven: If so be that being clothed we shall not be found naked. For we that are in this tabernacle do groan, being burdened: not for that we would be unclothed, but clothed upon, that mortality might be swallowed up of life. Now he that hath wrought us for the selfsame thing is God, who also hath given unto us the earnest of the Spirit.

—2 Corinthians 5:1-5

The LORD is my shepherd; I shall not want. He maketh me to lie down in green pastures: he leadeth me beside the still waters. He restoreth my soul: he leadeth me in the paths of righteousness for his name's sake. Yea, thou I walk through the valley of the shadow of death, I will fear no evil: for thou art with me; thy rod and thy staff they comfort me. Thou preparest a table before me in the presence of mine enemies: thou anointest my head with oil; my cup runneth over. Surely goodness and mercy shall follow me all the days of my life: and I will dwell in the house of the LORD for ever.

—Psalm 23

O give thanks unto the LORD; for he is good: because his mercy endureth for ever. Let Israel now say, that his mercy endureth for ever. Let the house of Aaron now say, that his mercy endureth for ever. Let them now that fear the LORD say, that his mercy endureth for ever. I called upon the LORD in distress: the LORD answered me, and set me in a large place. The LORD is on my side; I will not fear: what can man do unto me? The LORD taketh my part with them that help me: therefore shall I see my desire upon them that hate me. It is better to trust in the LORD than to put confidence in man.

—Psalm 118:1-8

Therefore being justified by faith, we have peace with God through our Lord Jesus Christ: By whom also we have access by faith into this grace wherein we stand,

and rejoice in hope of the glory of God. And not only so, but we glory in tribulations also: knowing that tribulation worketh patience; And patience, experience; and experience, hope: And hope maketh not ashamed; because the love of God is shed abroad in our hearts by the Holy Ghost which is given unto us.

—Romans 5:1-5

Seeing then that we have a great high priest, that is passed into the heavens, Jesus the Son of God, let us hold fast our profession. For we have not an high priest which cannot be touched with the feeling of our infirmities; but was in all points tempted like as we are, yet without sin. Let us therefore come boldly unto the throne of grace, that we may obtain mercy, and find grace to help in time of need.

—Hebrews 4:14-16

Is any among you afflicted? let him pray. Is any merry? let him sing psalms. Is any sick among you? let him call for the elders of the church; and let them pray over him, anointing him with oil in the name of the Lord: And the prayer of faith shall save the sick, and the Lord shall raise him up; and if he have committed sins, they shall be forgiven him. Confess your faults one to another, and pray one for another, that ye may be healed. The effectual fervent prayer of a righteous man availeth much. Elias was a man subject to like passions as we are, and he prayed earnestly that it might not rain: and it rained not on the earth by the space of three years and six months. And he prayed again, and the heaven gave rain, and the earth brought forth her fruit.

—James 5:13-18

Whosoever believeth that Jesus is the Christ is born of God: and every one that loveth him that begat loveth him also that is begotten of him. By this we know that we love the children of God, when we love God, and keep his commandments. For this is the love of God, that we keep his commandments: and his commandments are not grievous. For whatever is born of God overcometh the world: and this is the victory that overcometh the world, even our faith. Who is he that overcometh the world, but he that believeth that Jesus is the Son of God?

—1 John 5:1-5

Non-Christians Who Are Sick

Seek ye the LORD while he may be found, call ye upon him while he is near: Let the wicked forsake his way, and the unrighteous man his thoughts: and let him return unto the LORD, and he will have mercy upon him; and to our God, for he will abundantly pardon.

—Isaiah 55:6-7

For God so loved the world, that he gave his only begotten Son, that whosoever believeth in him should not perish, but have everlasting life. For God sent not his Son into the world to condemn the world; but that the world through him might be saved.

—John 3:16-17

Repent ye therefore, and be converted, that your sins may be blotted out, when the times of refreshing shall come from the presence of the Lord.

—Acts 3:19

For by grace are ye saved through faith; and that not of yourselves: it is the gift of God: Not of works, lest any man should boast. For we are his workmanship, created in Christ Jesus unto good works, which God hath before ordained that we should walk in them.

—Ephesians 2:8-10

If we receive the witness of men, the witness of God is greater: for this is the witness of God which he hath testified of his Son. He that believeth on the Son of God hath the witness in himself: he that believeth not God hath made him a liar; because he believeth not the record that God gave of his Son. And this is the record, that God hath given to us eternal life, and this life is in his Son. He that hath the Son hath life; and he that hath not the Son of God hath not life. These things have I written unto you that believe on the name of the Son of God; that ye may know that ye have eternal life, and that ye may believe on the name of the Son of God.

—1 John 5:9-13

Behold, I stand at the door, and knock: if any man hear my voice, and open the door, I will come in to him, and will sup with him, and he with me.

—Revelation 3:20

And the Spirit and the bride say, Come. And let him that heareth say, Come. And let him that is athirst come. And whosoever will, let him take the water of life freely.

—Revelation 22:17

20

Comforting Scripture for the Bereaved

Seeing then that we have a great high priest, that is passed into the heavens, Jesus the Son of God, let us hold fast our profession. For we have not an high priest which cannot be touched with the feeling of our infirmities; but was in all points tempted like as we are, yet without sin. Let us therefore come boldly unto the throne of grace, that we may obtain mercy, and find grace to help in time of need.

—Hebrews 4:14-16

But ye are come unto mount Zion, and unto the city of the living God, the heavenly Jerusalem, and to an innumerable company of angels. To the general assembly and church of the firstborn, which are written in heaven, and to God the Judge of all, and to the spirits of just men made perfect, and to Jesus the mediator of the new covenant, and to the blood of sprinkling, that speaketh better things than that of Abel . ... Wherefore seeing we also are compassed about with so great a cloud of witnesses, let us lay aside every weight, and the sin which doth so easily beset us, and let us run with patience the race that is set before us, Looking unto Jesus the author and finisher of our faith; who for the joy that was set before him endured the cross, despising the shame, and is set down at the right hand of the throne of God.

—Hebrews 12:22-24; 12:1- 2

He that dwelleth in the secret place of the most High shall abide under the shadow of the Almighty. I will say of the LORD, He is my refuge and my fortress: my God; in him will I trust . . . . For he shall give his angels charge over thee, to keep thee in all thy ways. They shall bear thee up in their hands, lest thou dash thy foot against a stone.

—Psalm 91:1-2, 11-12

My son, despise not the chastening of the LORD; neither be weary of his correction: for whom the LORD loveth he correcteth; even as a father the son in whom he delighteth.

—Proverbs 3:11-12

Leave thy fatherless children, I will preserve them alive; and let thy widows trust in me.

—Jeremiah 49:11

Precious in the sight of the LORD is the death of his saints.

—Psalm 116:15

Blessed is the man whom thou chastenest, O LORD, and teachest him out of thy law; That thou mayest give him rest from the days of adversity, until the pit be digged for the wicked. For the LORD will not cast off his people, neither will he forsake his inheritance.

—Psalm 94:12-14

Behold, happy is the man whom God correcteth: therefore despise not thou the chastening of the Almighty: For he maketh sore, and bindeth up: he woundeth, and his hands make whole. He shall deliver thee in six troubles: yea, in seven there shall no evil touch thee.

—Job 5:17-19

There hath no temptation taken you but such as is common to man: but God is faithful, who will not suffer you to be tempted above that ye are able; but will with the temptation also make a way to escape, that ye may be able to bear it.

—1 Corinthians 10:13

Beloved, think it not strange concerning the fiery trial which is to try you, as though some strange thing happened unto you: but rejoice, inasmuch as ye are partakers of Christ's sufferings; that, when his glory shall be revealed, ye may be glad also with exceeding joy.

—1 Peter 4:12-13

Blessed be God, even the Father of our Lord Jesus Christ, the Father of mercies, and the God of all comfort; Who comforteth us in all our tribulation, that we may be able to comfort them which are in any trouble, by the comfort wherewith we ourselves are comforted of God. For as the sufferings of Christ abound in us, so our consolation also aboundeth by Christ. And whether we be afflicted, it is for your consolation and salvation, which is effectual in the enduring of the same sufferings which we also suffer: or whether we be comforted, it is for your consolation and salvation. And our hope of you is stedfast, knowing, that as ye are partakers of the sufferings, so shall ye be also of the consolation.

—2 Corinthians 1:3-7

For I am in a strait betwixt two, having a desire to depart, and to be with Christ; which is far better.

—Philippians 1:23

And one of the elders answered, saying unto me, What are these which are arrayed in white robes? and whence came they? And I said unto him, Sir, thou knowest. And he said to me, These are they which came out of great tribulation, and have washed their robes, and made them white in the blood of the Lamb. Therefore are they before the throne of God, and serve him day and night in his temple: and he that sitteth on the throne shall dwell among them. They shall hunger no more, neither thirst any more; neither shall the sun light on them, nor any heat. For the Lamb who is in the midst of the throne shall feed them, and shall lead them unto living fountains of waters: and God shall wipe away all tears from their eyes.

—Revelation 7:13-17

For we know that if our earthly house of this tabernacle were dissolved, we have a building of God, an house not made with hands, eternal in the heavens. For in this we groan, earnestly desiring to be clothed upon with our house which is from heaven: If so be that being clothed we shall not be found naked. For we that are in this tabernacle do groan, being burdened: not for that we would be unclothed, but clothed upon, that mortality might be swallowed up of life. Now he that hath wrought us for the selfsame thing is God, who also hath given unto us the earnest of the Spirit. Therefore we are always confident, knowing that, whilst we are at home in the body, we are absent from the Lord: (for we walk by faith, not by sight:) we are confident, I say, and willing rather to be absent from the body, and to be present with the Lord. Wherefore we labour, that, whether present or absent, we may be accepted of him.

—2 Corinthians 5:1-9

For our conversation is in heaven; from whence also we look for the Saviour, the Lord Jesus Christ: Who shall change our vile body, that it may be fashioned like unto his glorious body, according to the working whereby he is able even to subdue all things unto himself.

—Philippians 3:20-21

And I heard a voice from heaven saying unto me, Write, Blessed are the dead which die in the Lord from henceforth: Yea, saith the Spirit, that they may rest from their labours; and their works do follow them.

—Revelation 14:13

The LORD is my strength and song, and he is become my salvation: he is my God, and I will prepare him an habitation; my father's God, and I will exalt him.

—Exodus 15:2

Let the words of my mouth, and the meditation of my heart, be acceptable in thy sight, O LORD, my strength, and my redeemer.

—Psalm 19:14

Many are the afflictions of the righteous: but the LORD delivereth him out of them all.

—Psalm 34:19

I sought the Lord, and he heard me, and delivered me from all my fears.

—Psalm 34:4

These things I have spoken unto you, that in me ye might have peace. In the world ye shall have tribulation: but be of good cheer; I have overcome the world.

—John 16:33

Thou wilt shew me the path of life: in thy presence is fulness of joy; at thy right hand there are pleasures for evermore.

—Psalm 16:11

In my Father's house are many mansions: if it were not so, I would have told you. I go to prepare a place for you.

—John 14:2

But my God shall supply all your need according to his riches in glory by Christ Jesus.

—Philippians 4:19

The steps of a good man are ordered by the Lord: and he delighteth in his way. Though he fall, he shall not be utterly cast down: for the Lord upholdeth him with his hand.

—Psalm 37:23-24

If ye abide in me, and my words abide in you, ye shall ask what ye will, and it shall be done unto you.

—John 15:7

Thou shalt guide me with thy counsel, and afterward receive me to glory.

—Psalm 73:24

In all thy ways acknowledge him, and he shall direct thy paths.

—Proverbs 3:6

They that sow in tears shall reap in joy. He that goeth forth and weepeth, bearing precious seed, shall doubtless come again with rejoicing, bringing his sheaves with him.

—Psalm 126:5-6

Finally, brethren, whatsoever things are true, whatsoever things are honest, whatsoever things are just, whatsoever things are pure, whatsoever things are lovely, whatsoever things are of good report; if there be any virtue, and if there be any praise, think on these things.

—Philippians 4:8

The Lord is my rock, and my fortress, and my deliverer; my God, my strength, in whom I will trust; my buckler, and the horn of my salvation, and my high tower.

—Psalm 18:2

Cast thy burden upon the Lord, and he shall sustain thee: he shall never suffer the righteous to be moved.

—Psalm 55:22

Every good gift and every perfect gift is from above, and cometh down from the Father of lights, with whom is no variableness, neither shadow of turning.

—James 1:17

Thou shalt not be afraid for the terror by night; nor for the arrow that flieth by day . ... A thousand shall fall at thy side, and ten thousand at thy right hand; but it shall not come nigh thee.

—Psalm 91:5, 7

But thou, when thou prayest, enter into thy closet, and when thou hast shut thy door, pray to the Father which is in secret; and thy Father which seeth in secret shall reward thee openly.

—Matthew 6:6

And the ransomed of the LORD shall return, and come to Zion with songs and everlasting joy upon their heads: they shall obtain joy and gladness, and sorrow and sighing shall flee away.

—Isaiah 35:10

Why art thou cast down, O my soul? and why art thou disquieted within me? hope in God: for I shall yet praise him, who is the health of my countenance, and my God.

—Psalm 43:5

For ye have not received the spirit of bondage again to fear; but ye have received the Spirit of adoption, whereby we cry, Abba, Father. The Spirit itself beareth witness with our spirit, that we are the children of God: And if children, then heirs; heirs of God, and joint-heirs with Christ; if so be that we suffer with him, that we may be also glorified together. For I reckon that the sufferings of this present time are not worthy to be compared with the glory which shall be revealed in us.

—Romans 8:15-18

Come unto me, all ye that labour and are heavy laden, and I will give you rest. Take my yoke upon you, and learn of me; for I am meek and lowly in heart: and ye shall find rest unto your souls. For my yoke is easy, and my burden is light.

—Matthew 11:28-30

The LORD is my shepherd; I shall not want. He maketh me to lie down in green pastures: he leadeth me beside the still waters. He restoreth my soul: he leadeth me in the paths of righteousness for his name's sake. Yea, though I walk through the valley of the shadow of death, I will fear no evil: for thou art with me; thy rod and thy staff they comfort me. Thou preparest a table before me in the presence of mine enemies: thou anointest my head with oil; my cup runneth over. Surely goodness and mercy shall follow me all the days of my life: and I will dwell in the house of the LORD for ever.

—Psalm 23

And he said unto me, My grace is sufficient for thee: for my strength is made perfect in weakness. Most gladly therefore will I rather glory in my infirmities, that the power of Christ may rest upon me.

—2 Corinthians 12:9

Beloved, now are we the sons of God, and it doth not yet appear what we shall be: but we know that, when he shall appear, we shall be like him; for we shall see him as he is.

—1 John 3:2

The arms of his hands were made strong by the hands of the mighty God of Jacob.

—Genesis 49:24

I will seek that which was lost, and bring again that which was driven away, and will bind up that which was broken, and will strengthen that which was sick.

—Ezekiel 34:16

Hast thou not known? hast thou not heard, that the everlasting God, the LORD, the Creator of the ends of the earth, fainteth not, neither is weary? there is no searching of his understanding. He giveth power to the faint; and to them that have no might he increaseth strength. Even the youths shall faint and be weary, and the young men shall utterly fall: But they that wait upon the LORD shall renew their strength; they shall mount up with wings as eagles; they shall run, and not be weary; and they shall walk, and not faint.

—Isaiah 40:28-31

Come now, and let us reason together, saith the LORD: though your sins be as scarlet, they shall be as white as snow; though they be red like crimson, they shall be as wool.

—Isaiah 1:18

Therefore being justified by faith, we have peace with God through our Lord Jesus Christ: By whom also we have access by faith into this grace wherein we stand, and rejoice in hope of the glory of God.

—Romans 5:1-2

As the mountains are round about Jerusalem, so the LORD is round about his people from henceforth even for ever.

—Psalm 125:2

What time I am afraid, I will trust in thee.

—Psalm 56:3

Many sorrows shall be to the wicked: but he that trusteth in the LORD, mercy shall compass him about.

—Psalm 32:10

21
Funeral Service

The minister, standing at the head of the casket or some other appropriate place, may begin the service by reading one or more of the following passages.

"I am the resurrection and the life: he that believeth in me, though he were dead, yet shall he live: And whosoever liveth and believeth in me shall never die" (John 11:25-26).

"Let not your heart be troubled: ye believe in God, believe also in me. In my Father's house are many mansions: if it were not so, I would have told you. I go to prepare a place for you. And if I go and prepare a place for you, I will come again, and receive you unto myself; that where I am, there ye may be also . . . Let not your heart be troubled, neither let it be afraid" (John 14:1-3, 27).

"For I know that my redeemer liveth, and that he shall stand at the latter day upon the earth . . . Whom I shall see for myself, and mine eyes shall behold, and not another" (Job 19:25, 27).

Prayer

Hymn

Sung by choir, soloist, or a selected group.

Scripture

One or more of the following passages may be used. Others may be selected from the section titled "*Scripture Selections to Be Used at Funerals.*"

LORD, thou hast been our dwelling place in all generations. Before the mountains were brought forth, or ever thou hadst formed the earth and the world, even from everlasting to everlasting, thou art God. Thou turnest man to destruction; and sayest, Return, ye children of men. For a thousand years in thy sight are but as yesterday when it is past, and as a watch in the night. Thou carriest them away as with a flood; they are as a sleep: in the morning they are like grass which groweth up. In the morning it flourisheth, and groweth up; in the evening it is cut down, and withereth. For we are consumed by thine anger, and by thy wrath are we troubled. Thou hast set our iniquities before thee, our secret sins in the light of thy countenance. For all our days are passed away in thy wrath: we spend our years as a tale that is told. The days of our years are threescore years and ten; and if by reason of strength they be fourscore years, yet is their strength labour and sorrow; for it is soon cut off, and we fly away. Who knoweth the power of thine anger? even according to thy fear, so is thy wrath. So teach us to number our days, that we may apply our hearts unto wisdom. Return, O LORD, how long? and let it repent thee concerning thy servants. O satisfy us early with thy mercy; that we may rejoice and be glad all our days. Make us glad according to the days wherein thou hast afflicted us, and the years wherein we have seen evil. Let thy work appear unto thy servants, and thy glory unto their children. And let the beauty of the LORD our God be upon us: and establish thou the work of our hands upon us: yea, the work of our hands establish thou it.

—Psalm 90

The LORD is my light and my salvation; whom shall I fear? the LORD is the strength of my life; of whom shall I be afraid? When the wicked, even mine enemies and my foes, came upon me to eat up my flesh, they stumbled and fell. Though an host should encamp against me, in this will I be confident. One thing have I desired of the LORD, that will I seek after; that I may dwell in the house of the LORD all the days of my life, to behold the beauty of the LORD, and to inquire in his temple. For in the time of trouble he shall hide me in his pavilion: in the secret of his tabernacle shall he hide me; he shall set me up upon a rock. And now shall mine head be lifted up above mine enemies round about me: therefore will I offer in his tabernacle sacrifices of joy; I will sing, yea, I will sing praises unto the LORD. Hear, O LORD, when I cry with my voice: have mercy also upon me, and answer me. When thou saidst, Seek ye my face; my heart said unto thee, Thy face, LORD, will I seek. Hide not thy face far from me; put not thy servant away in anger: thou hast been my help; leave me not, neither forsake me, O God of my salvation. When my father and my mother forsake me, then the LORD will take me up. Teach me thy way, O LORD, and lead me in a plain path, because of mine enemies. Deliver me not over unto the will of mine enemies: for false witnesses are risen up against me, and such as breathe out cruelty. I had fainted, unless I had believed to see the goodness of the LORD in the land of the living. Wait on the LORD: be of good courage, and he shall strengthen thine heart: wait, I say, on the LORD.

—Psalm 27

All flesh is not the same flesh: but there is one kind of flesh of men, another flesh of beasts, another of fishes, and another of birds. There are also celestial bodies, and bodies terrestrial: but the glory of the celestial is one, and the glory of the terrestrial is another. There is one glory of the sun, and another glory of the moon, and another glory of the stars: for one star differeth from another star in glory. So also is the resurrection of the dead. It is sown in corruption; it is raised in incorruption: It is sown in dishonour it is raised in glory: it is sown in weakness; it is raised in power: It is sown a natural body; it is raised a spiritual body. There is a natural body, and there is a spiritual body. And so it is written, The first man Adam was made a living soul; the last Adam was made a quickening spirit. Howbeit that was not first which is spiritual, but that which is natural; and afterward that which is spiritual. The first man is of the earth, earthy: the second man is the Lord from heaven. As is the earthy, such are they also that are earthy: and as is the heavenly, such are they also that are heavenly. And as we have borne the image of the earthy, we shall also bear the image of the heavenly. Now this I say, brethren, that flesh and blood cannot inherit the kingdom of God; neither doth corruption inherit incorruption. Behold, I shew you a mystery; We shall not all sleep, but we shall all be changed. In a moment, in the twinkling of an eye, at the last trump: for the trumpet shall sound, and the dead shall be raised incorruptible, and we shall be changed. For this corruptible must put on incorruption, and this mortal must put on immortality. So when this corruptible shall have put on incorruption, and this mortal shall have put on immorality, then shall be brought to pass the saying that is written, Death is swallowed up in victory. O death, where is thy sting? O grave, where is thy victory? The sting of death is sin; and the strength of sin is the law. But thanks be to God, which giveth us the victory through our Lord Jesus Christ. Therefore, my beloved brethren, be ye stedfast, unmoveable, always abounding in the work of the Lord, forasmuch as ye know that your labour is not in vain in the Lord.

—1 Corinthians 15:39-58

Hymn

Sung by choir, soloist, or a selected group.

Address or remarks

Benediction

The peace of God which passeth all understanding keep your hearts and minds in the knowledge and love of God, and of His Son, Jesus Christ, our Lord. Amen.

22

Scripture Selections to Be Used at Funerals

Opening Scripture

God is our refuge and strength, a very present help in trouble. Therefore will we not fear, though the earth be removed, and though the mountains be carried into the midst of the sea; Though the waters thereof roar and be troubled, though the mountains shake with the swelling thereof.

—Psalm 46:1-3

For I know that my Redeemer liveth, and that he shall stand at the latter day upon the earth: And though after my skin worms destroy this body, yet in my flesh shall I see God: Whom I shall see for myself, and mine eyes shall behold, and not another.

—Job 19:25-27

I am the resurrection, and the life: he that believeth in me, though he were dead, yet shall he live: And whosoever liveth and believeth in me shall never die.

—John 11:25-26

These things I have spoken unto you, that in me ye might have peace. In the world ye shall have tribulation: but be of good cheer; I have overcome the world.

—John 16:33

Blessed be God, even the Father of our Lord Jesus Christ, the Father of mercies, and the God of all comfort; Who comforteth us in all our tribulation, that we may be able to comfort them which are in any trouble, by the comfort wherewith we ourselves are comforted of God.

—2 Corinthians 1:3-4

For thou hast been a strength to the poor, a strength to the needy in his distress, a refuge from the storm, a shadow from the heat, when the blast of the terrible ones is as a storm against the wall.

—Isaiah 25:4

When thou passeth through the waters, I will be with thee; and through the rivers, they shall not overflow thee: when thou walkest through the fire, thou shalt not be burned; neither shall the flame kindle upon thee.

—Isaiah 43:2

For our light affliction, which is but for a moment, worketh for us a far more exceeding and eternal weight of glory; While we look not at the things which are seen, but at the things which are not seen, for the things which are seen are temporal; but the things which are not seen are eternal.

—2 Corinthians 4:17-18

Behold, what manner of love the Father hath bestowed upon us, that we should be called the sons of God: therefore the world knoweth us not, because it knew him not. Beloved, now are we the sons of God, and it doth not yet appear what we shall be: but we know that, when he shall appear, we shall be like him: for we shall see him as he is.

—1 John 3:1-2

Verily, verily, I say unto you, The hour is coming, and now is, when the dead shall hear the voice of the Son of God: and they that hear shall live.

—John 5:25

And this is the will of him that sent me, that every one which seeth the Son, and believeth on him, may have everlasting life: and I will raise him up at the last day.

— John 6:40

I am the living bread which came down from heaven: if any man eat of this bread he shall live forever: and the bread that I will give is my flesh, which I will give for the life of the world.

John 6:51

For the Funeral of a Child

The Lord is my shepherd; I shall not want. He maketh me to lie down in green pastures: he leadeth me beside the still waters. He restoreth my soul: he leadeth me in the paths of righteousness for his name's sake. Yea, though I walk through the valley of the shadow of death, I will fear no evil: for thou art with me; thy rod and thy staff they comfort me. Thou preparest a table before me in the presence of mine enemies: thou anointest my head with oil; my cup runneth over. Surely goodness and mercy shall follow me all the days of my life: and I will dwell in the house of the LORD for ever.

—Psalm 23

At the same time came the disciples unto Jesus, saying, Who is the greatest in the kingdom of heaven? And Jesus called a little child unto him, and set him in the midst of them, And said, Verily I say unto you, Except ye be converted, and become as little children, ye shall not enter into the kingdom of heaven. Whosoever therefore shall humble himself as this little child, the same is the greatest in the kingdom of heaven. And whoso shall receive one such little child in my name receiveth me . . . Take heed that ye despise not one of these little ones; for I say unto you, That in heaven their angels do always behold the face of my Father which is in heaven.

—Matthew 18:1-5, 10

So she went and came unto the man of God to mount Carmel. And it came to pass, when the man of God saw her afar off, that he said to Gehazi his servant, Behold, yonder is that Shunammite: Run now, I pray thee, to meet her, and say unto her, Is it well with thee? is it well with thy husband? is it well with the child? And she answered, It is well.

—2 Kings 4:25-26

David therefore besought God for the child; and David fasted, and went in, and lay all night upon the earth. And the elders of his house arose and went to him, to raise him up from the earth: but he would not, neither did he eat bread with them. And it came to pass on the seventh day, that the child died. And the servants of David feared to tell him that the child was dead: for they said, Behold, while the child was yet alive, we spake unto him, and he would not hearken unto our voice: how would he then vex himself, if we tell him that the child is dead? But when David saw that his servants whispered, David perceived that the child was dead: therefore David said unto his servants, Is the child dead? And they said, He is dead. Then David arose from the earth, and washed, and anointed himself, and changed his apparel, and came into the house of the LORD, and worshipped: then he came to his own house; and when he required, they set bread before him, and he did eat. Then said his servants unto him, What thing is this that thou hast done? thou didst fast and weep for the child, while it was alive; but when the child was dead, thou didst rise and eat bread. And he said, While the child was yet alive, I fasted and wept: for I said, Who can tell whether God will be gracious to me, that the child may live? But now he is dead, wherefore should I fast? can I bring him back again? I shall go to him, but he shall not return to me.

—2 Samuel 12:16-23

And they brought young children to him, that he should touch them: and his disciples rebuked those that brought them. But when Jesus saw it, he was much displeased, and said unto them, Suffer the little children to come unto me, and forbid them not: for of such is the kingdom of God. Verily I say unto you, Whosoever shall not receive the kingdom of God as a little child, he shall not enter therein. And he took them up in his arms, put his hands upon them, and blessed them.

—Mark 10:13-16

Take heed that ye despise not one of these little ones; for I say unto you, That in heaven their angels do always behold the face of my Father which is in heaven. For the Son of man is come to save that which was lost. How think ye? if a man have an hundred sheep, and one of them be gone astray, doth he not leave the ninety and nine, and goeth into the mountains, and seeketh that which is gone astray? And if so be that he find it, verily I say unto you, he rejoiceth more of that sheep, than of the ninety and nine which went not astray. Even so it is not the will of your Father which is in heaven, that one of these little ones should perish.

—Matthew 18:10-14

They shall hunger no more, neither thirst any more; neither shall the sun light on them, nor any heat. For the Lamb which is in the midst of the throne shall feed them, and shall lead them unto living fountains of waters: and God shall wipe away all tears from their eyes.

—Revelation 7:16-17

For the Funeral of a Youth

In the morning sow thy seed, and in the evening withhold not thine hand: for thou knowest not whether shall prosper, either this or that, or whether they both shall be alike good. Truly the light is sweet, and a pleasant thing it is for the eyes to behold the sun: But if a man live many years, and rejoice in them all; yet let him remember the days of darkness; for they shall be many. All that cometh is vanity. Rejoice, O young man, in thy youth; and let thy heart cheer thee in the days of thy youth, and walk in the ways of thine heart, and in the sight of thine eyes:

but know thou, that for all these things God will bring thee into judgment. Therefore remove sorrow from thy heart, and put away evil from thy flesh: for childhood and youth are vanity.

—Ecclesiastes 11:6-10

Remember now thy Creator in the days of thy youth, while the evil days come not, nor the years draw nigh, when thou shalt say, I have no pleasure in them; While the sun, or the light, or the moon, or the stars, be not darkened, nor the clouds return after the rain: In the day when the keepers of the house shall tremble, and the strong men shall bow themselves, and the grinders cease because they are few, and those that look out of the windows be darkened, And the doors shall be shut in the streets, when the sound of the grinding is low, and he shall rise up at the voice of the bird, and all the daughters of musick shall be brought low; Also when they shall be afraid of that which is high, and fears shall be in the way, and the almond tree shall flourish, and the grasshopper shall be a burden, and desire shall fail: because man goeth to his long home, and the mourners go about the streets: Or ever the silver cord be loosed, or the golden bowl be broken, or the pitcher be broken at the fountain, or the wheel broken at the cistern. Then shall the dust return to the earth as it was: and the spirit shall return unto God who gave it.

—Ecclesiastes 12:1-7

And it came to pass the day after, that he went into a city called Nain; and many of his disciples went with him, and much people. Now when he came nigh to the gate of the city, behold, there was a dead man carried out, the only son of his mother, and she was a widow: and much people of the city was with her. And when the Lord saw her, he had compassion on her, and said unto her, Weep not. And he came and touched the bier: and they that bare him stood still. And he said, Young man, I say unto thee, Arise. And he that was dead sat up, and began to speak. And he delivered him to his mother. And there came a fear on all: and they glorified God, saying, That a great prophet is risen up among us; and, That God hath visited his people.

—Luke 7:11-16

For the Funeral of a Godly Woman

Hear my prayer, O Lord, and let my cry come unto thee. Hide not thy face from me in the day when I am in trouble; incline thine ear unto me: in the day when I call answer me speedily.

—Psalm 102:1-2

Like as a father pitieth his children, so the Lord pitieth them that fear him. For he knoweth our frame; he remembereth that we are dust. As for man, his days are as grass: as a flower of the field, so he flourisheth. For the wind passeth over it, and it is gone; and the place thereof shall know it no more. But the mercy of the Lord is from everlasting to everlasting upon them that fear him, and his righteousness unto children's children; to such as keep his covenant, and to those that remember his commandments to do them.

—Psalm 103:13-18

Then saith Martha unto Jesus, Lord, if thou hadst been there, my brother had not died. But I know, that even now, whatsoever thou wilt ask of God, God will give it thee. Jesus saith unto her, Thy brother shall rise again. Martha saith unto him, I know that he shall rise again in the resurrection at the last day. Jesus said unto her, I am the resurrection and the life: he that believeth in me, though he were dead, yet shall he live: And whosoever liveth and believeth in me shall never die. Believest thou this?

—John 11:21-26

Now there was at Joppa a certain disciple named Tabitha, which by interpretation is called Dorcas: this woman was full of good works and almsdeeds which she did. And it came to pass in those days, that she was sick, and died: whom when they had washed, they laid her in an upper chamber. And forasmuch as Lydda was nigh to Joppa, and the disciples had heard that Peter was there, they sent unto him two men, desiring him that he would not delay to come to them. Then Peter arose and went with them. When he was come, they brought him into the upper chamber: and all the widows stood by him weeping, and shewing the coats and garments which Dorcas made, while she was with them. But Peter put them all forth, and kneeled down, and prayed; and turning him to the body said, Tabitha, arise. And she opened her eyes: and when she saw Peter, she sat up. And he gave her his hand, and lifted her up; and when he had called the saints and widows, presented her alive. And it was known throughout all Joppa; and many believed in the Lord.

—Acts 9:36-42

When Jesus understood it, he said unto them, Why trouble ye the woman: for she hath wrought a good work upon me. For ye have the poor always with you; but me ye have not always. For in that she hath poured this ointment on my body, she did it for my burial. Verily I say unto you, Wheresoever this gospel shall be preached in the whole world, there shall also this, that this woman hath done, be told for a memorial of her.

—Matthew 26:10-13

Now upon the first day of the week, very early in the morning, they came unto the sepulchre, bringing the spices which they had prepared, and certain others with them. And they found the stone rolled away from the sepulchre. And they entered in, and found not the body of the Lord Jesus. And it came to pass, as they were much perplexed thereabout, behold, two men stood by them in shining garments: And as they were afraid, and bowed down their faces to the earth, they said unto them, Why seek ye the living among the dead? He is not here, but is risen: remember how he spake unto you when he was yet in Galilee, Saying, the Son of man must be delivered into the hands of sinful men, and be crucified, and the third day rise again. And they remembered his words, And returned from the sepulchre, and told all these things unto the eleven, and to all the rest. It was Mary Magdalene, and Joanna, and Mary the mother of James, and other women that were with them, which told these things unto the apostles.

—Luke 24:1-10

Let not your heart be troubled: ye believe in God, believe also in me. In my Father's house are many mansions: if it were not so, I would have told you. I go to prepare a place for you. And if I go and prepare a place for you, I will come again, and receive you unto myself; that where I am, there ye may be also . . . . Peace I leave with you, my peace I give unto you: not as the world giveth, give I unto you. Let not your heart be troubled, neither let it be afraid.

—John 14:1-3, 27

Blessed are they that do his commandments, that they may have right to the tree of life, and may enter in through the gates into the city.

—Revelation 22:14

For the Funeral of Those of Mature Years

God is our refuge and strength, a very present help in trouble. Therefore will not we fear, though the earth be removed, and though the mountains be carried into the midst of the sea; Though the waters thereof roar and be troubled, though the mountains shake with the swelling thereof. There is a river, the streams whereof shall make glad the city of God, the holy place of the tabernacles of the most High. God is in the midst of her; she shall not be moved: God shall help her, and that right early . . . . Be still, and know that I am God: I will be exalted among the heathen, I will be exalted in the earth. The Lord of hosts is with us; the God of Jacob is our refuge.

—Psalm 46:1-5, 10-11

Come unto me, all ye that labour and are heavy laden, and I will give you rest.

—Matthew 11:28

I will lift up mine eyes unto the hills, from whence cometh my help. My help cometh from the LORD, which made heaven and earth. He will not suffer thy foot to be moved: he that keepeth thee will not slumber. Behold, he that keepeth Israel shall neither slumber nor sleep. The LORD is thy keeper: the LORD is thy shade upon thy right hand. The sun shall not smite thee by day, nor the moon by night. The LORD shall preserve thee from all evil: he shall preserve thy soul. The LORD shall preserve thy going out and thy coming in from this time forth, and even for evermore.

—Psalm 121

Beloved, think it not strange concerning the fiery trial which is to try you, as though some strange thing happened unto you: But rejoice, inasmuch as ye are partakers of Christ's sufferings; that, when his glory shall be revealed, ye may be glad also with exceeding joy. If ye be reproached for the name of Christ, happy are ye; for the spirit of glory and of God resteth upon you: on their part he is evil spoken of, but on your part he is glorified.

—1 Peter 4:12-14

And Enoch walked with God: and he was not; for God took him.

—Genesis 5:24

And thou shalt go to thy fathers in peace; thou shalt be buried in a good old age.

—Genesis 15:15

The hoary head is a crown of glory, if it be found in the way of righteousness.

—Proverbs 16:31

And even to your old age I am he; and even to hoar hairs will I carry you: I have made, and I will bear; even I will carry, and will deliver you.

—Isaiah 46:4

For I am now ready to be offered, and the time of my departure is at hand. I have fought a good fight, I have finished my course, I have kept the faith: Henceforth, there is laid up for me a crown of righteousness, which the Lord, the righteous judge, shall give me at that day: and not to me only, but unto all them also that love his appearing.

—2 Timothy 4:6-8

After this I beheld, and, lo, a great multitude, which no man could number, of all nations, and kindreds, and people, and tongues, stood before the throne, and before the Lamb, clothed with white robes, and palms in their hands; And cried with a loud voice, saying, Salvation to our God which sitteth upon the throne, and unto the Lamb. And all the angels stood round about the throne, and about the elders and the four beasts, and fell before the throne on their faces, and worshipped God, Saying, Amen: Blessing, and glory, and wisdom, and thanksgiving and honour, and power, and might, be unto our God for ever and ever. Amen. And one of the elders answered, saying unto me, What are these which are arrayed in white robes? And whence came they? And I said unto him, Sir, thou knowest. And he said to me, These are they which came out of great tribulation, and have washed their robes, and made them white in the blood of the Lamb. Therefore are they before the throne of God, and serve him day and night in his temple: and he that sitteth on the throne shall dwell among them. They shall hunger no more, neither thirst any more; neither shall the sun light on them, nor any heat. For the Lamb which is in the midst of the throne shall feed them, and shall lead them unto living fountains of waters: and God shall wipe away all tears from their eyes.

—Revelation 7:9-17

23
Funeral Texts

General

But now he is dead, wherefore should I fast? can I bring him back again? I shall go to him, but he shall not return to me.

—2 Samuel 12:23

Yet in my flesh shall I see God.

—Job 19:26

Commit thy way unto the Lord; trust also in him; and he shall bring it to pass.

—Psalm 37:5

Come unto me, all ye that labour and are heavy laden, and I will give you rest.

—Matthew 11:28

He will swallow up death in victory; and the Lord God will wipe away tears from off all faces.

—Isaiah 25:8

But God will redeem my soul from the power of the grave: for he shall receive me.

—Psalm 49:15

Thine eyes shall see the king in his beauty: they shall behold the land that is very far off.

—Isaiah 33:17

And the ransomed of the LORD shall return, and come to Zion with songs and everlasting joy upon their heads: they shall obtain joy and gladness, and sorrow and sighing shall flee away.

—Isaiah 35:10

Leave thy fatherless children, I will preserve them alive; and let thy widows trust in me.

—Jeremiah 49:11

I will ransom them from the power of the grave; I will redeem them from death: O death, I will be thy plagues; O grave, I will be thy destruction: repentance shall be hid from mine eyes.

—Hosea 13:14

Seek him that maketh the seven stars and Orion, and turneth the shadow of death into the morning, and maketh the day dark with night: that calleth for the waters of the sea, and poureth them out upon the face of the earth: The LORD is his name.

—Amos 5:8

Then shall the righteous shine forth as the sun in the kingdom of their Father.

—Matthew 13:43

He that believeth on the Son hath everlasting life: and he that believeth not the Son shall not see life; but the wrath of God abideth on him.

—John 3:36

Verily, verily, I say unto you, He that heareth my word, and believeth on him that sent me, hath everlasting life, and shall not come into condemnation; but is passed from death unto life.

—John 5:24

Jesus said unto her, I am the resurrection, and the life: he that believeth in me, though he were dead, yet shall he live: And whosoever liveth and believeth in me shall never die. Believest thou this?

—John 11:25-26

In my Father's house are many mansions: if it were not so, I would have told you. I go to prepare a place for you. And if I go and prepare a place for you, I will come again, and receive you unto myself; that where I am, there ye may be also.

—John 14:2-3

Father, I will that they also, whom thou hast given me, be with me where I am; that they may behold my glory, which thou hast given me: for thou lovedst me before the foundation of the world.

—John 17:24

For I reckon that the sufferings of this present time are not worthy to be compared with the glory which shall be revealed in us.

—Romans 8:18

But as it is written, Eye hath not seen, nor ear heard, neither have entered into the heart of man, the things which God hath prepared for them that love him.

—1 Corinthians 2:9

For our light affliction, which is but for a moment, worketh for us a far more exceeding and eternal weight of glory.

—2 Corinthians 4:17

For we know that if our earthly house of this tabernacle were dissolved, we have a building of God, an house not made with hands, eternal in the heavens.

—2 Corinthians 5:1

To an inheritance incorruptible, and undefiled, and that fadeth not away, reserved in heaven for you.

—2 Peter 1:4

And the world passeth away, and the lust thereof: but he that doeth the will of God abideth for ever.

—1 John 2:17

And this is the promise that he hath promised us, even eternal life.

—1 John 2:25

I am he that liveth, and was dead; and, behold, I am alive for evermore, . . . and have the keys of hell and of death.

—Revelation 1:18

For Children

And he returned unto his brethren, and said, The child is not; and I, whither shall I go?

—Genesis 37:30

But now he is dead, wherefore should I fast? can I bring him back again? I shall go to him, but he shall not return to me.

—2 Samuel 12:23

The LORD gave, and the LORD hath taken away; blessed be the name of the LORD.

—Job 1:21

He shall gather the lambs with his arm, and carry them in his bosom.

—Isaiah 40:11

And they shall be mine, saith the LORD of hosts, in that day when I make up my jewels; and I will spare them, as a man spareth his own son that serveth him.

—Malachi 3:17

In Rama was there a voice heard, lamentation, and weeping, and great mourning, Rachel weeping for her children, and would not be comforted, because they are not.

—Matthew 2:18

But Jesus said, Suffer little children, and forbid them not, to come unto me: for of such is the kingdom of heaven.

—Matthew 19:14

For Young People

How are the mighty fallen in the midst of the battle! O Jonathan, thou wast slain in thine high places.

—2 Samuel 1:25

And as he went, thus he said, O my son Absalom, my son, my son Absalom! would God I had died for thee, O Absalom, my son, my son!

—2 Samuel 18:33

Remember now thy Creator in the days of thy youth.

—Ecclesiastes 12:1

Her sun is gone down while it was yet day.

—Jeremiah 15:9

How is the strong staff broken, and the beautiful rod!

—Jeremiah 48:17

Now when he came nigh to the gate of the city, behold, there was a dead man carried out, the only son of his mother, and she was a widow.

—Luke 7:12

Martha saith unto him, I know that he shall rise again in the resurrection at the last day.

—John 11:24

For Those of Mature Years

And Enoch walked with God: and he was not; for God took him.

—Genesis 5:24

And thou shalt go to thy fathers in peace; thou shalt be buried in a good old age.

—Genesis 15:15

And Jacob said unto Pharaoh, The days of the years of my pilgrimage are an hundred and thirty years: few and evil have the days of the years of my life been, and have not attained unto the days of the years of the life of my fathers in the days of their pilgrimage.

—Genesis 47:9

And Israel said unto Joseph, Behold, I die: but God shall be with you, and bring you again unto the land of your fathers.

—Genesis 48:21

Nevertheless I am continually with thee: thou hast holden me by my right hand. Thou shalt guide me with thy counsel, and afterward receive me to glory.

—Psalm 73:23-24

The days of our years are threescore years and ten; and if by reason of strength they be fourscore years, yet is their strength labour and sorrow; for it is soon cut off, and we fly away.

—Psalm 90:10

24
Committal Service I

At the grave, the body having been placed and the people assembled, the minister may say:

But I would not have you to be ignorant, brethren, concerning them which are asleep, that ye sorrow not, even as others which have no hope. For if we believe that Jesus died and rose again, even so them also which sleep in Jesus will God bring with Him. For this we say unto you by the word of the Lord, that we which are alive and remain unto the coming of the Lord shall not prevent them which are asleep. For the Lord Himself shall descend from heaven with a shout, with the voice of the archangel, and with the trump of God: and the dead in Christ shall rise first: Then we which are alive and remain shall be caught up together with them in the clouds, to meet the Lord in the air: and so shall we ever be with the Lord. Wherefore comfort one another with these words.

And I heard a voice from heaven saying unto me, Write, Blessed are the dead which die in the Lord from henceforth: Yea, saith the Spirit, that they may rest from their labours; and their works do follow them.

Committal

Since Almighty God, in His providence, has taken from this life the soul of our deceased (brother, sister) we therefore commit (his, her) body to the grave and entrust (his, her) spirit to Him who gave it. For we know that if our earthly house of this tabernacle be dissolved, we have a building of God, an house not made with hands, eternal in the heavens.

Committal Prayer

In the minister's own words or the following:

Almighty God, our loving heavenly Father, who brought back from the dead our Lord Jesus Christ, that great Shepherd of the sheep: grant, as we stand beside the grave of our departed (brother, sister), that the voice which spoke to the women at the tomb may speak to us also, saying: "He whom thou seekest is not here; He is risen and goeth before thee." When the sense of sorrow and loneliness weighs heavily upon us, and the shadows deepen, and faith falters, and hope grows dim, draw us closer to You, O God; enfold us in Your love, sustain us by Your grace, and keep us ever loyal to the blessed memories of this solemn hour, until the night is past, and with the morning we are united with those we have loved and lost; through Jesus Christ our Lord. Amen.

Benediction

The grace of our Lord Jesus Christ, and the love of God, and the communion of the Holy Spirit, be with us all, evermore. Amen.

25
Committal Service II

At the grave, the body having been placed and the people assembled, the minister may say:

Now this I say, brethren, that flesh and blood cannot inherit the kingdom of God; neither doth corruption inherit incorruption. Behold, I shew you a mystery; We shall not all sleep, but we shall all be changed, In a moment, in the twinkling of an eye, at the last trump: for the trumpet shall sound, and the dead shall be raised incorruptible, and we shall be changed. For this corruptible must put on incorruption, and this mortal must put on immortality. So when this corruptible shall have put on incorruption, and this mortal shall have put on immortality, then shall be brought to pass the saying that is written, Death is swallowed up in victory. O death, where is thy sting? O grave where is thy victory? The sting of death is sin; and the strength of sin is the law. But thanks be to God, which giveth us the victory through our Lord Jesus Christ. Therefore, my beloved brethren, be ye steadfast, unmoveable, always abounding in the work of the Lord, forasmuch as ye know that your labour is not in vain in the Lord.

For our light affliction, which is but for a moment, worketh for us a far more exceeding and eternal weight of glory; While we look not at the things which are seen, but at the things which are not seen: for the things which are seen are temporal; but the things which are not seen are eternal. For we know that if our earthly house of this tabernacle were dissolved, we have a building of God, an house not made with hands, eternal in the heavens.

Committal

Unto the mercy of Almighty God, we commend the soul of our departed (brother, sister) and commit (his, her) body to the ground, earth to earth, ashes to ashes, dust to dust, in the sure and certain hope of the resurrection from the dead, through Jesus Christ our Lord.

Blessed are the dead which die in the Lord from henceforth: Yea, saith the Spirit, that they may rest from their labours; and their works do follow them.

Committal Prayer

In the minister's own words or the following:

Almighty God, who by the death of Your dear Son, Jesus Christ, has destroyed death; and by His rest in the tomb has sanctified the graves of the saints, and by His glorious resurrection has brought life and immortality to light, we humbly thank You for that victory over death and the grave which He has obtained for us and for all who have died in Him. Keep us in everlasting fellowship with all who wait for You and in union with Him who is the Resurrection and the Life, who lives and reigns with You and the Holy Spirit, ever one God, forever and ever. Amen.

Benediction

Now the God of peace, that brought again from the dead our Lord Jesus, that great Shepherd of the sheep, through the blood of the everlasting covenant, make you perfect in every good work to do His will, working in you that which is well pleasing in His sight, through Jesus Christ; to whom be glory forever and ever. Amen.

26
Committal Service III

At the grave, the body having been placed and the people assembled, the minister may say:

Man that is born of woman is of few days and full of trouble. He cometh forth like a flower; and is cut down: he fleeth also as a shadow, and continueth not.

All flesh is grass, and all the goodliness thereof is as the flower of the field: The grass withereth, the flower fadeth ... but the word of our God shall stand forever.

As a father pitieth his children, so the Lord pitieth them that fear Him. For He knoweth our frame; He remembereth that we are dust. As for man, his days are as grass: as a flower of the field, so he flourisheth. For the wind passeth over it, and it is gone; and the place thereof shall know it no more.

Committal

Since Almighty God, in His wise providence, has permitted the removal of the soul of the departed, we therefore commit the body to the grave and the spirit to God who gave it, in the assurance that He who is the Judge of all the earth shall do right.

Committal Prayer

Benediction

The Lord bless you, and keep you; the Lord make His face shine upon you, and be gracious unto you; the Lord lift up His countenance upon you, and give you peace. Amen.

27

Committal Service for a Child

At the grave, the body having been placed and the people assembled, the minister may say:

Hear the words of our Lord: Blessed are they that mourn: for they shall be comforted.

Let not your heart be troubled, neither let it be afraid.

Suffer the little children to come unto Me and forbid them not for of such is the kingdom of heaven.

Hear also the words of the apostle Paul:

But some man will say, How are the dead raised up? and with what body do they come? That which thou sowest is not quickened, except it die: And that which thou sowest, thou sowest not that body that shall be, but bare grain, it may chance of wheat, or of some other grain: But God giveth it a body as it hath pleased Him, and to every seed his own body. ... So also is the resurrection of the dead. It is sown in corruption; it is raised in incorruption: It is sown in dishonour; it is raised in glory: it is sown in weakness; it is raised in power: It is sown a natural body; it is raised a spiritual body. There is a natural body, and there is a spiritual body.

Committal

In the faith of our Lord Jesus Christ, who took little children in His arms and blessed them, we commit to the ground the body of this dear child, in the assurance that (his, her) immortal spirit is at home with (his, her) Heavenly Father.

They shall be Mine, saith the Lord of hosts, in that day when I make up My jewels.

Committal Prayer

Almighty God, our Heavenly Father: We thank You for the love that cares for us in life and watches over us in death. May we in faith and hope give back to You the life which in love was given us. We bless Your name for our Savior's joy in little children and for the assurance that of such is the kingdom of heaven. We believe that in death as in life they are in His holy keeping. In our sorrow make us strong to commit ourselves and those we love to Your never-failing care. In our perplexity may we trust where we cannot understand, knowing that the eternal God is our Refuge and underneath are the everlasting arms. In our loneliness make our remembrance grateful and may we never forget that You will keep that which we have committed, until the eternal morning breaks; through Jesus Christ our Lord. Amen.

Benediction

O Lord, support us all the day long, until the shadows lengthen and the evening comes, and the busy world is hushed, and the fever of life is over, and our work is done. Then in Your mercy grant us a safe lodging, a holy rest, and peace at the last; through Jesus Christ our Lord. Amen.

28

Ground Breaking Ceremony

Before building a new church building it is fitting to hold a service on the ground where the church will be erected. The leaders of the community should be invited to share with the congregation in this service.

Invocation

Hymn

Scripture

Therefore whosoever heareth these sayings of mine, and doeth them, I will liken him unto a wise man, which built his house upon a rock: And the rain descended and the floods came and the winds blew, and beat upon that house; and it fell not: for it was founded upon a rock. And everyone that heareth these sayings of mine, and doeth them not, shall be likened unto a foolish man, which built his house upon the sand: And the rain descended, and the floods came, and the winds blew, and beat upon that house; and it fell: and great was the fall of it.

—Matthew 7:24-27

Prayer

Special Music

Remarks

In the minister's own words or the following:

The Word of God informs us that except the Lord build the house they labor in vain who build it. One of the Lord's servants of earlier years said, "How amiable are Thy tabernacles, O LORD, of Hosts! My soul longeth, yea, even fainteth for the courts of the LORD. And my flesh crieth out for the Living God."

We rejoice together in the prospect of breaking ground for a building to be erected to the glory of God. It is our glad hope that this spot may indeed be holy ground where many may find a demonstration of the revelation and the blessing of Jehovah. May this occasion help us to break up the hard ground of our hearts, knowing it is time to seek the Lord. We also trust that this act may symbolize for us the planting of the good seed of the kingdom in good soil looking toward a bountiful harvest. As we plan to build may we be continually reminded that we are laborers together with God.

Whereas we are constituted as a people of God, believers in the Lord Jesus Christ, who is our Savior and Lord, and conscious of His commissioning us to be His witnesses, we therefore proceed to take this first step in our building program.

We will now turn the sod on which we stand that here there may be erected a temple to His praise, a permanent witness to the people, a house of worship, a place for spiritual nourishment and inspiration as we grow together in Christ.

At this time three designated individuals will take shovel in hand and turn a sizable piece of sod. In order, the sod will be turned in the name of the Father . . . the Son . . . and the Holy Spirit. Following this, others may turn a shovelful of earth as desired. The minister then continues:

Now that we have taken the first step toward the erection of this building, may there be a prayer in all of our hearts that the blessings of God may accompany our progress in the completion of this building and bring us all to the day of it's dedication, to the honor and glory of God.

Hymn

Benediction

29

Laying of Church Cornerstone

The audience having assembled at the site and those officiating taken their places, the minister will say:

My beloved church family and friends: God spoke to Moses, the man of God, and commanded that a tabernacle be set up in the wilderness. This tabernacle was constructed under divine direction for worship by the Jews. The blessings of the Father of the universe rested upon King Solomon in building the Temple, which is known in history as being the greatest architectural work ever designed. David, under divine instructions, furnished this design, the plan, and the location for this wonderful building. It was erected for the worship of Almighty God. Therefore, as God moved Moses, David, and Solomon to erect places to be used for the assembling of those who would worship Him, that same God has moved our hearts to build this structure for a similar purpose.

Doxology

Scripture

Then David said, This is the house of the Lord God, and this is the altar of the burnt offering for Israel. And

David commanded to gather together the strangers that were in the land of Israel; and he set masons to hew wrought stones to build the house of God. And David prepared iron in abundance for the nails for the doors of the gates, and for the joinings; and brass in abundance without weight; Also cedar trees in abundance: for the Zidonians and they of Tyre brought much cedar wood to David. And David said, Solomon my son is young and tender, and the house that is to be builded for the LORD must be exceeding magnifical, of fame and of glory throughout all countries: I will therefore now make preparation for it. So David prepared abundantly before his death. Then he called for Solomon his son, and charged him to build an house for the LORD God of Israel. And David said to Solomon, My son, as for me, it was in my mind to build an house unto the name of the LORD my God: But the word of the LORD came to me, saying, Thou hast shed blood abundantly, and hast made great wars: thou shalt not build an house unto my name, because thou hast shed much blood upon the earth in my sight. Behold, a son shall be born to thee, who shall be a man of rest; and I will give him rest from all his enemies round about: for his name shall be Solomon, and I will give peace and quietness unto Israel in his days. He shall build an house for my name; and he shall be my son, and I will be his father; and I will establish the throne of his kingdom over Israel for ever. Now, my son, the LORD be with thee; and prosper thou, and build the house of the LORD thy God, as he hath said of thee. Only the LORD give thee wisdom and understanding, and give thee charge concerning Israel, that thou mayest keep the law of the LORD thy God. Then shalt thou prosper, if thou takest heed to fulfill the statutes and judgments which the LORD charged Moses with concerning Israel: be strong, and of good courage; dread not, nor be dismayed. Now, behold, in my trouble I have prepared for the house of the LORD an hundred thousand talents of gold, and a thousand thousand talents of silver; and of brass and iron without weight; for it is in abundance: timber also and stone have I prepared; and thou mayest add thereto. Moreover there are workmen with thee in abundance, hewers and workers of stone and timber, and all manner of cunning men for every manner of work. Of the gold, the silver, and the brass, and the iron, there is no number. Arise therefore, and be doing, and the LORD be with thee. David also commanded all the princes of Israel to help Solomon his son, saying, Is not the LORD your God with you? and hath he not given you rest on every side? for he hath given the inhabitants of the land into mine hand; and the land is subdued before the LORD, and before his people. Now set your heart and your soul to seek the LORD your God; arise therefore, and build ye the sanctuary of the LORD God, to bring the ark of the covenant of the LORD, and the holy vessels of God, into the house that is to be built to the name of the LORD.

—1 Chronicles 22

Hymn

Prayer

In the minister's own words or the following:

Most Holy God, let Your blessing rest on those who labor in building this house; shield them from all harm, and grant to them, and all of us, Your heavenly grace, that our gifts and all our service may be set apart for You, and that we may conduct ourselves as the living temples of the Holy Spirit. Amen.

Address

> *At the conclusion of the address, the minister shall display the stone and read the list of contents. Then with the assistance of the builder, the minister will deposit the stone. This being done, the minister will strike the stone three times with a trowel and say:*

In the name of the Father, and of the Son, and of the Holy Spirit, we lay this cornerstone in the foundation of this building. May the blessings of God rest upon the building and completion of the building, and may it be dedicated for the worship of God, and for a spiritual home for His children while journeying to that house not made with hands eternal in the heavens. Amen.

Hymn

Benediction

Behold, bless ye the LORD, all ye servants of the LORD which by night stand in the house of the LORD. Lift up your hands in the sanctuary, and bless the LORD. The LORD that made heaven and earth bless thee out of Zion. Amen.

—Psalm 134

30

Dedication of Church

The following is a recommended order of service to be used either at the regular worship service or at a special Service of Dedication.

Organ Prelude

Call to Worship

Hymn

Scripture Lesson

Now, my God, let, I beseech thee, thine eyes be open, and let thine ears be attent unto the prayer that is made in this place. Now therefore arise, O LORD God, into thy resting place, thou, and the ark of thy strength: let thy priests, O LORD God, be clothed with salvation, and let thy saints rejoice in goodness.

—2 Chronicles 6:40-41

Lift up your heads, O ye gates; and be ye lift up, ye everlasting doors; and the King of glory shall come in. Who is this King of glory? The LORD strong and mighty, the LORD mighty in battle. Lift up your heads, O ye gates; even lift them up, ye everlasting doors; and the King of glory shall come in. Who is this King of glory? The LORD of hosts, he is the King of glory. Selah.

—Psalm 24:7-10

How amiable are thy tabernacles, O LORD of hosts! My soul longeth, yea, even fainteth for the courts of the LORD: my heart and my flesh crieth out for the living God. Yea, the sparrow hath found an house, and the swallow a nest for herself, where she may lay her young, even thine altars, O LORD of hosts, my King, and my God. Blessed are they that dwell in thy house: they will be still praising thee. Selah. Blessed is the man whose strength is in thee; in whose heart are the ways of them. Who passing through the valley of Baca make it a well; the rain also filleth the pools. They go from strength to strength, every one of them in Zion appeareth before God. O LORD God of hosts, hear my prayer: give ear, O God of Jacob. Selah. Behold, O God our shield, and look upon the face of thine anointed. For a day in thy courts is better than a thousand. I had rather be a doorkeeper in the house of my God, than to dwell in the tents of wickedness. For the LORD God is a sun and shield: the LORD will give grace and glory: no good thing will he withhold from them that walk uprightly. O LORD of hosts, blessed is the man that trusteth in thee.

—Psalm 84:1-12

For the LORD hath chosen Zion; he hath desired it for his habitation. This is my rest for ever: here will I dwell; for I have desired it. I will abundantly bless her provision: I will satisfy her poor with bread. I will also clothe her priests with salvation: and her saints shall shout aloud for joy.

—Psalm 132:13-16

In the year that king Uzziah died I saw also the LORD sitting upon a throne, high and lifted up, and his train filled the temple. Above it stood the seraphims: each one had six wings; with twain he covered his face, and with twain he covered his feet, and with twain he did fly. And one cried unto another, and said, Holy, holy, holy, is the LORD of hosts: the whole earth is full of his glory.

—Isaiah 6:1-3

Prayer

The Offering

Anthem or Hymn

Message

Presentation of the Keys

The Chairman of the Building Committee shall say to the Minister:

The Building Committee has completed the work that was assigned to it by the congregation. I, therefore, as Chairman of the Building Committee, present to you the keys to the building.

Then shall the minister say:

It is fitting at this special occasion to bow in worship before the Lord our God. The Most High does not dwell in temples made with hands, yet He commanded His servant Moses to build a tabernacle, and prepare a place for Him where a manifestation of His presence would dwell. At the dedication of the tabernacle, and afterwards at the dedication of the temple, God sanctioned and confirmed the work by the revelation of His glory, and blessed His people there. Our Lord has also given us the blessed assurance that He will meet with His people wherever they assemble themselves in His name. Therefore, we know God will accept this house that we have built to His glory. Having this confidence, we now dedicate this house unto the Triune God: Father, Son, and Holy Spirit, to be His sanctuary, where His Word shall be preached, the ordinances administered, and other services held as He leads this church.

To this end we also dedicate ourselves to Him, with all that we are and possess, without reservation, to be His through the grace of Jesus Christ our Lord.

*The Act of Dedication**

*See end of service for alternate "Act of Dedication."

The people will stand and join in the responses.

Minister

We set apart this facility to the worship of the living and true God, and to the service of Jesus Christ our Lord.

Congregation

We devote it to the preaching of the Gospel for the conversion of sinners, and to the education of Christians in the knowledge of spiritual truth for all the activities of Christian life.

Minister

The incense of prayer and praise will ascend to God here. The ordinances of the Lord's house will be sacredly observed here.

Congregation

The Word of God, which lives and abides forever, will be sounded out here for the salvation of the lost, and shine as a perpetual light to guide God's people to everlasting life.

Minister

May children of sin and sorrow find a refuge here from despair and ruin, and Christians find a safe place here when trials come.

Congregation

May no conflict or strife ever be heard within these walls, no unholy spirit of pride or worldliness find entrance here.

Minister

And may God graciously accept this offering of a house in His name—an offering made by grateful hearts and willing hands—and bless every heart that shares in this gift.

Congregation

May many come to know God here, so that when all of us have gone to be with the Lord, others will take up the service until Christ shall come and take all His saints home.

Minister

To the glory of God, our Father, by whose favor we have built; to the honor of Jesus the Christ, the Son of the living God and our Savior; to the praise of the Holy Spirit, source of life and light.

Congregation

We dedicate this house.

Minister

To the sanctification of the family; to the training and nurture of children; to the inspiration of youth and the salvation of all.

Congregation

We dedicate this house.

Minister

To the help of the needy; to the promotion of Christian brotherhood; to the extension of the kingdom through the whole wide world.

Congregation

We dedicate this house.

Dedication Prayer

In the minister's own words or the following:

Lord God of our fathers, Your people have built this house for Your worship and glory. You who are above all the heavens and fill the immensity of space with Your greatness and presence, we pray that You accept it in the name of Your Son our Savior. You did dwell in the temple of old, and wherever two or three are gathered in Your name, You are in the midst of Your people. May this house be preserved from all unholy purposes and exercises, and be devoted to Your service alone, and to the redemption and building up of mankind, through Jesus Christ our Lord. Amen.

Transfer of Keys

The minister shall now ask the Board of Trustees to appear before him and shall say:

The Building Committee of this church has completed their work. By this act of transfer of the keys, they commit to you, the Trustees of this church, the responsibility of caring for this building.

I charge you, as members of the Trustee Board, with the responsibility given to you by this church.

As you accept these keys, do you accept the accompanying responsibilities?

Response

We do.

Hymn

Benediction

Now unto Him that is able to do exceeding abundantly above all that we ask or think, according to the power that worketh in us, unto Him be glory in the Church by Christ Jesus throughout all ages, world without an end. Amen.

**Acts of Dedication (Alternate)*

Minister

To the glory of God our Father, by whose favor we have built this house; To the honor of Jesus, the Christ, the Son of the living God, our Lord and Savior; to the praise of the Holy Spirit, source of life and light.

People

We dedicate this house.

Minister

For worship and prayer and song; for the ministry of the Word; for the celebration of the ordinances of the Church.

People

We dedicate this house.

Minister

For comfort for those who mourn; for strength to those who are tempted; for help in right living.

People

We dedicate this house.

Minister

For the sanctification of the family; for the guidance of children; for the salvation of men.

People

We dedicate this house.

Minister

For standing against evil; for fostering patriotism; for promoting civic righteousness.

People

We dedicate this house.

Minister

For sympathy and fellowship with the needy; for brotherhood with all men; for the essential unity of all believers in Jesus Christ.

People

We dedicate this house.

Minister

For missionary endeavor at home and abroad; for worldwide evangelism and education, till all the kingdoms of the world become the kingdom of our Lord and of His Christ; for the reform of social wrongs, till all human society is transformed by the power of the gospel.

People

We dedicate this house.

Minister

In grateful memory of all who have loved and served this church; with hearts eager to see again those who have departed from this earthly life; a free-will offering of thanksgiving and praise.

People

We dedicate this house.

Minister and People

We, the people of this church and congregation, surrounded by a great cloud of witnesses, grateful for our heritage, remembering the sacrifices of our fathers and mothers, confessing that apart from us their work cannot be completed, do dedicate ourselves anew to the worship of God and Christian service to others.

31

Dedication of Educational Building

A suggested service for incorporation with a regular order of worship.

Declaration

It is with an awareness of God's grace and the cooperation of each other that we are privileged to see this completed structure. We believe this building to be evidence of God's blessing upon the efforts of those who have worked diligently to see it completed.

This educational center will provide facilities and opportunities for passing on the treasures of our Christian faith to this and future generations. Here the Bible will be taught. Here inquiring minds will be exposed to truth, and hearts to Him who is the Truth. Here all of life will be measured by the written and the Incarnate Word so that each life may be lived with purpose and that Christ might be formed within us.

We give thanks to God for His guiding wisdom, abounding strength, and divine aid in this enterprise. We thank Him for those who by their gifts and service have made this building a reality. Let us all with one voice sing our praises to God in the name of Jesus Christ.

The congregation will then unite in singing "The Church's One Foundation" or another appropriate hymn.

Scripture

Suggested portions:

Blessed are the undefiled in the way, who walk in the law of the LORD. Blessed are they that keep his testimonies, and that seek him with the whole heart. They also do no iniquity: they walk in his ways. Thou hast commanded us to keep thy precepts diligently.

—Psalm 119:1-4

Happy is the man that findeth wisdom, and the man that getteth understanding. For the merchandise of it is better than the merchandise of silver, and the gain thereof than fine gold. She is more precious than rubies: and all the things thou canst desire are not to be compared unto her. Length of days is in her right hand; and in her left hand riches and honour. Her ways are ways of pleasantness, and all her paths are peace. She is a tree of life to them that lay hold upon her: and happy is every one that retaineth her.

—Proverbs 3:13-18

Therefore whosoever heareth these sayings of mine, and doeth them, I will liken him unto a wise man, which built his house upon a rock: And the rain descended, and the floods came, and the winds blew, and beat upon that house; and it fell not: for it was founded upon a rock. And every one that heareth these sayings of mine, and doeth them not, shall be likened unto a foolish man, which built his house upon the sand: And the rain descended, and the floods came, and the winds blew, and beat upon that house; and it fell: and great was the fall of it.

—Matthew 7:24-27

Responsive Reading

Minister

Wisdom hath builded her house, she hath hewn out her seven pillars.

Congregation

Doth not wisdom cry? and understanding put forth her voice?

Minister

She standeth in the top of high places, by the way in the places of the paths.

Congregation

She crieth at the gates, at the entry of the city, at the coming in at the doors.

Minister

Unto you, O men, I call; and my voice is to the sons of man.

Congregation

O ye simple, understand wisdom: and, ye fools, be ye of an understanding heart.

Minister

Hear; for I will speak of excellent things; and the opening of my lips shall be right things.

Congregation

For my mouth shall speak truth; and wickedness is an abomination to my lips.

Minister

Receive my instruction, and not silver; and knowledge rather than choice gold.

Congregation

For wisdom is better than rubies; and all the things that may be desired are not to be compared to it.

Minister

But where shall wisdom be found? and where is the place of understanding?

Congregation

Behold, the fear of the Lord, that is wisdom; and to depart from evil is understanding.

Then the trustees or the proper committee shall deliver the keys to the minister in the presence of the congregation, and one of them should say:

This building is presented to you, to be dedicated to the service of Almighty God for the enlightenment of His people.

While the people stand the minister shall say:

Buildings erected for ministry in the name of our Lord and Savior Jesus Christ should be formally set apart for their special uses. We would not only dedicate this building, but also those who gave gifts and service. Now, we give ourselves anew to the service of God; our labor, that it may be according to God's holy will; our bodies, that they may be suitable temples for the indwelling of the Holy Spirit; our souls, that they may be renewed in the image of Christ.

Minister

In the name of God: the Father, the Son, and the Holy Spirit, we dedicate this building to the holy ministry of Christian education. Let all the people say:

Congregation

Amen.

Minister

We dedicate this building to the continual search for abundant life that is in Christ, both for each individual and for the world. May all that is done within these walls be done to the honor and glory of God. Let all the people say:

Congregation

Amen.

Prayer

In the minister's own words or the following:

Merciful Father, guide at all times the thoughts and the efforts of Your people, so that Your purpose will always be fulfilled in their lives. Allow them all to know that which is worth knowing, to love that which is worth loving, to praise that which pleases You most. Give them true judgment to distinguish truth from error, courage to turn away from all that is evil, and strength to do all those things which we know to be right in Your sight; through Jesus Christ our Lord. Amen.

Benediction

Now unto Him that is able to keep you from falling, and to present you faultless before the presence of His glory with exceeding joy, to the only wise God our Savior, be glory and majesty, dominion and power, both now and forever. Amen.

32

Mortgage or Note Burning

This ceremony may be a part of the Sunday morning worship service. The minister may appropriately preach a sermon relative to the subject of Christian stewardship.

At the place in the service when the mortgage is to be burned, the trustees should be invited to appear before the officiating minister. In lieu of the mortgage, a facsimile may be used in the ceremony.

Remarks by the Chairman of the Board of Trustees

Under the blessing of God, we have arrived at this hour. Through the sacrifice and dedication of this church family the last dollar of indebtedness has been paid. We now present the mortgage to you to be burned. This is a day of victory and achievement. Let us give thanks to God and rejoice in it.

Response by Minister

I rejoice with you that through the devotion and generosity of this congregation the debt of this church has been paid. I believe the faithfulness, loyalty, and generosity of each member is very pleasing to our heavenly Father. This facility is an expression of your love for God. With gratitude and thankfulness in our hearts, we give praise to God. This should mark the beginning of even greater service for this church in the work of God's kingdom.

Here the minister lights a candle, passing it to the chosen person who ignites the mortgage. As this takes place the minister shall read as follows:

Praise ye the LORD. Praise God in his sanctuary: praise him in the firmament of his power. Praise him for his mighty acts: praise him according to his excellent greatness. Praise him with the sound of the trumpet: praise him with the psaltery and harp. Praise him with the timbrel and dance: praise him with stringed instruments and organs. Praise him upon the loud cymbals: praise him upon the high sounding cymbals. Let every thing that hath breath praise the LORD. Praise ye the LORD.

—Psalm 150

While the mortgage is being consumed "The Doxology" may be sung.

Benediction

33

Scriptural Benedictions

The LORD bless you, and keep you; the LORD make his face to shine upon you, and be gracious unto you; the LORD lift up his countenance upon you, and give you peace. Amen. (See Numbers 6:24-26.)

Behold, bless ye the LORD, all ye servants of the LORD, which by night stand in the house of the LORD. Lift up your hands in the sanctuary, and bless the LORD. The LORD that made heaven and earth bless thee out of Zion.

—Psalm 134:1-3

And now, brethren, I commend you to God, and to the word of his grace, which is able to build you up, and to give you an inheritance among all them which are sanctified.

—Acts 20:32

Now the God of patience and consolation grant you to be like-minded one toward another according to Christ Jesus: That ye may with one mind and one mouth glorify God, even the Father of our Lord Jesus Christ."

—Romans 15:5-6

Now the God of hope fill you with all joy and peace in believing, that ye may abound in hope, through the power of the Holy Ghost.

—Romans 15:13

The grace of our Lord Jesus Christ be with you all. Amen.

—Romans 16:24

Grace be unto you, and peace, from God our Father, and from the Lord Jesus Christ, now and forever. Amen.

—1 Corinthians 1:3

The Lord Jesus Christ be with thy spirit. Grace be with you. Amen.

—2 Timothy 4:22

Grace, mercy and peace, from God our Father, and Jesus Christ our Lord, be and abide with you all forever. Amen.

—1 Timothy 1:2

And the peace of God, which passeth all understanding, shall keep your hearts and minds through Christ Jesus; for ever and ever. Amen.

—Philippians 4:7

But the God of all grace, who hath called us unto his eternal glory by Christ Jesus, after that ye have suffered a while, make you perfect, establish, strengthen, settle you. To him be glory and dominion for ever and ever. Amen.

—1 Peter 5:10-11

But grow in grace, and in the knowledge of our Lord and Saviour Jesus Christ. To him be glory both now and forever. Amen.

—2 Peter 3:18

Unto him that loved us, and washed us from our sins in his own blood, And hath made us kings and priests unto God and his Father; to him be glory and dominion for ever and ever. Amen.

—Revelation 1:5-6

The grace of the Lord Jesus Christ, and the love of God, and the communion of the Holy Ghost, be with you all. Amen.

—2 Corinthians 13:14

Now unto him that is able to do exceeding abundantly above all that we ask or think, according to the power that worketh in us, Unto him be glory in the church by Christ Jesus throughout all ages, world without end. Amen.

—Ephesians 3:20-21

Now the God of peace, that brought again from the dead our Lord Jesus, that great shepherd of the sheep, through the blood of the everlasting covenant, Make you perfect in every work to do his will, working in you that which is well pleasing in his sight, through Jesus Christ; to whom be glory for ever and ever. Amen.

—Hebrews 13:20-21

Now unto him that is able to keep you from falling, and to present you faultless before the presence of his glory with exceeding joy, To the only wise God our Saviour, be glory and majesty, dominion and power, both now and ever. Amen.

—Jude 24-25

34
Selected Poetry

FROM THANATOPSIS

So live, that when thy summons comes to join
The innumerable caravan, which moves
To that mysterious realm, where each shall take
His chamber in the silent halls of death,
Thou go not, like the quarry-slave at night,
Scourged to his dungeon, but, sustained and soothed
By an unfaltering trust, approach thy grave,
Like one who wraps the drapery of his couch
About him and lies down to pleasant dreams.

—William Cullen Bryant

THREE WORDS OF STRENGTH

There are three lessons I would write,
Three words as with a burning pen,
In tracings of eternal light,
Upon the hearts of men.
Have hope. Though clouds environ round,
And gladness hides her face in scorn,
Put thou the shadow from thy brow—
No night but has its morn.
Have faith. Where'er thy bark is driven—
The calm's disport, the tempest's mirth—
Know this: God rules the host of heaven,
The inhabitants of the earth.

Have love. Not love alone for one,
    But man as man thy brother call;
And scatter, like a circling sun,
    Thy charities on all.
Thus grave these lessons upon thy soul—
    Hope, faith, and love—and thou shalt find
Strength when life's surges rudest roll,
    Light, when thou else wert blind.

—Schiller

"AND HE CALLED A LITTLE CHILD"

Beyond the planets and the far-off stars
    Our little sister's ear heard God's clear call;
Life's sunny noon, its reddening sunset bars,
    And pleasant evening shades—she left them all.
So now "she never would know pain and sin"—
Such halting comfort we each other gave
When like a dove her soul had fluttered in
    High heaven's opening gate;
Yet standing by her waxen body in the grave
Endeavoring to quiet sorrow's din
    We wept—so desolate!
Lord, when the eternal summons comes for me
    To take the last lone stretch that ends life's day
Ere I the King in all His beauty see,
    With a rejoicing heart may I forget the way
So full of things I could not understand—
The griefs and dark crimes of a cruel world—
    And may I firmly hold with faithful hand,
If black the night and wild
The banner of Thy love aloft—unfurled,

That angels may when I before Thee stand
   Say, "He called a little child."

—Grace W. Haight

O FOR A FAITH THAT WILL NOT SHRINK

O for a faith that will not shrink,
Though pressed by every foe,
That will not tremble on the brink
Of any earthly woe!
That will not murmur nor complain
Beneath the chastening rod,
But, in the hour of grief or pain,
Will lean upon its God.
A faith that shines more bright and clear
When tempests rage without,
That when in danger knows no fear,
In darkness feels no doubt;
Lord, give us such a faith as this,
And then, whate'er may come,
We'll taste e'en here the hallowed bliss
Of the eternal home.

—William H. Bathurst

THE WEAVER

My life is but a weaving
   Between my Lord and me;
I may not choose the colors,
   He knows what they should be;
For He can view the pattern
   Upon the upper side,
While I can see it only

On this, the under side.
Sometimes He weaveth sorrow,
Which seems strange to me;
But I will trust His judgment,
And work as faithfully;
'Tis He who fills the shuttle,
He knows just what is best,
So I shall weave in earnest
And leave with Him the rest.
Not till the loom is silent
And the shuttles cease to fly
Shall God unroll the canvas
And explain the reason why—
The dark threads are as needful
In the weaver's skillful hand
As the threads of gold and silver
In the pattern He has planned.

—Anonymous

CROSSING THE BAR

Sunset and evening star,
And one clear call for me!
And may there be no moaning of the bar,
When I put out to sea,
But such a tide as moving seems asleep,
Too full for sound and foam,
When that which drew from out the boundless deep
Turns again home.
Twilight and evening bell,
And after that the dark!
And may there be no sadness of farewell,

When I embark;
For tho' from out our bourne of Time and Place
The flood may bear me far,
I hope to see my Pilot face to face
When I have crossed the bar.

—Alfred Tennyson

SOME TIME WE'LL UNDERSTAND

Now now, but in the coming years
It may be in the better land,
We'll read the meaning of our tears,
And there, some time, we'll understand.
We'll catch the broken thread again,
And finish what we here began;
Heav'n will the mysteries explain.
And then, ah, then, we'll Understand.
We'll know why clouds instead of sun
Were over many a cherished plan;
Why song has ceased when scarce begun;
'Tis there, some time, we'll understand.
God knows the way, He holds the key,
He guides us with unerring hand;
Some time with tearless eyes we'll see;
Yes, there, up there, we'll understand.
Then trust in God thro' all the days;
Fear not, for He doth hold thy hand;
Though dark thy way, still sing and praise,
Some time, some time, we'll understand.

—Maxwell N. Cornelius

SAFE IN THE ARMS OF JESUS

Safe in the arms of Jesus, safe on His gentle breast,
There by His love o'ershaded, sweetly my soul shall rest.
Hark! 'tis the voice of angels, borne in a song to me,
Over the fields of glory, over the jasper sea,
Safe in the arms of Jesus, safe from corroding care,
Safe from the world's temptations, sin cannot harm me there.
Free from the blight of sorrow, free from my doubts and fears; Only a few more trials, only a few more tears!
Jesus, my heart's dear refuge, Jesus has died for me;
Firm on the Rock of Ages, ever my trust shall be.
Here let me wait with patience, wait till the night is o'er;
Wait till I see the morning break on the golden shore.
Safe in the arms of Jesus, safe on His gentle breast,
There by His love o'ershaded, sweetly my soul shall rest.

—Fanny Crosby

JESUS, BLESSED JESUS

There's One Who can comfort when all else fails,
Jesus, blessed Jesus;
A Saviour Who saves tho' the foe assails,
Jesus, blessed Jesus:
Once He traveled the way we go,
Felt the pangs of deceit and woe;
Who more perfectly then can know,
Than Jesus, blessed Jesus?
He never forsakes in the darkest hour,
Jesus, blessed Jesus;
His arm is around us with keeping power,
Jesus, blessed Jesus:

When we enter the Shadowland,
When at Jordan we trembling stand,
He will meet us with outstretched hand,
This Jesus, blessed Jesus.
What joy it will be when we see His face,
Jesus, blessed Jesus;
Forever to sing of His love and grace,
Jesus, blessed Jesus:
There at home on that shining shore,
With the loved ones gone on before,
We will praise Him forevermore,
Our Jesus, blessed Jesus.

—Charles H. Gabriel

COME, YE DISCONSOLATE

Come, ye disconsolate, where'er ye languish,
Come to the mercy-seat, fervently kneel.
Here bring your wounded hearts, here tell your anguish;
Earth has no sorrow that heaven cannot heal.
Joy of the desolate, light of the straying,
Hope of the penitent, fadeless and pure!
Here speaks the Comforter, tenderly saying,
"Earth has no sorrows that heaven cannot cure."
Here see the Bread of Life; see the waters flowing
Forth from the throne of God, pure from above.
Come to the feast prepared; come, ever knowing
Earth has no sorrow but heaven can remove.

—Thomas Moore

THERE IS NO SORROW, LORD, TOO LIGHT

There is no sorrow, Lord, too light
To bring in prayer to Thee;
There is no anxious care too slight
To wake Thy sympathy.
Thou, who hast trod the thorny road,
Wilt share each small distress;
The love, which bore the greater load,
Will not refuse the less.
There is no secret sight we breathe,
But meets Thine ear divine;
And every cross grows light beneath
The shadow, Lord, of Thine.

—Jane Crewdson

SHOULD YOU GO FIRST

Should you go first and I remain,
  To walk the road alone,
I'll live in memory's garden, dear,
  With happy days we've known.
In Spring I'll wait for roses red,
  When fade the lilac blue;
In early Fall when brown leaves fall,
  I'll catch a glimpse of you.
Should you go first and I remain,
  For battles to be fought,
Each thing you've touched along the way
  Will be a hallowed spot.
I'll hear your voice, I'll see your smile,
  Though blindly I may grope,
The memory of your helping hand

Will buoy me with hope.
Should you go first and I remain,
To finish with the scroll,
No lengthening shadows shall creep in
To make this life seem droll.
We've known so much of happiness,
We've had our cup of joy,
And memory is one gift of God
That death cannot destroy.
Should you go first and I remain,
One thing I'd have to do:
Walk slowly down that long, lone path,
For soon I'll follow you.
I'll want to know each step you take
That I may walk the same,
For someday down that lonely road
You'll hear me call your name.

—Albert Rowswell

HOW BLEST THE RIGHTEOUS WHEN HE DIES

How blest the righteous when he dies!
When sinks a weary soul to rest,
How mildly beam the closing eyes,
How gently heaves the expiring breast!
So fades a summer cloud away;
So sinks the gale when storms are o'er;
So gently shuts the eye of day;
So dies a wave along the shore.
A holy quiet reigns around,
A calm which life not death destroys;
And naught disturbs that peace profound

Which his unfettered soul enjoys.
Life's labor done, as sinks the clay,
Light from its load the spirit flies,
While Heav'n and earth combine to say,
"How blest the righteous when he dies!"

—Anna Barbauld

IT IS NOT DEATH TO DIE

It is not death to die,
  To leave this weary road,
And midst the brotherhood on high
  To be at home with God.
It is not death to close
  The eye long dimmed by tears,
And wake, in glorious repose
  To spend eternal years.
It is not death to bear
  The wrench that sets us free
From dungeon chain, to breathe the air
  Of boundless liberty.
It is not death to fling
  Aside this sinful dust
And rise, on strong exulting wing
  To live among the just.
Jesus, Thou Prince of Life,
  Thy chosen cannot die:
Like Thee, they conquer in the strife
  To reign with Thee on high.

—H. A. Cesar Malan

WHAT GOD HATH PROMISED

God hath not promised
  Skies always blue,
Flower-strewn pathways
  All our lives through;
God hath not promised
  Sun without rain,
Joy without sorrow,
  Peace without pain.
But God hath promised
  Strength for the day,
Rest for the labor,
  Light for the way,
Grace for the trials,
  Help from above,
Unfailing sympathy,
  Undying love.

—Anne Johnson Flint

MARRIAGE CEREMONIES PERFORMED

NAME	DATE

MARRIAGE CEREMONIES PERFORMED

NAME	DATE

MARRIAGE CEREMONIES PERFORMED

NAME	DATE

FUNERAL SERVICES PERFORMED

NAME	DATE

FUNERAL SERVICES PERFORMED

NAME	DATE

FUNERAL SERVICES PERFORMED

NAME	DATE

FUNERAL SERVICES PERFORMED

NAME	DATE

BABY DEDICATIONS PERFORMED

NAME	DATE

BABY DEDICATIONS PERFORMED

NAME	DATE

BABY DEDICATIONS PERFORMED

NAME	DATE